GALLOPING THE GLOBE

The Geography Unit Study for Young Learners

Loreé Pettit & Dari Mullins

Published by Geography Matters, Inc.

Programs utilized during production: Serif Page Plus 8, Puzzle Power, Art Explosion, ClipTures volume 4

ISBN 978-1-931397-65-0

Library of Congress Control Number: 2010924938

Printed in the United States of America

Geography Matters, Inc.
800-426-4650
www.geomatters.com

Dedication

Galloping the Globe is lovingly dedicated to our children, Jason and Aaron Pettit as well as Artie, Autumn, and Aspen Mullins. The five of you are the biggest blessings in our lives. We are so thankful that God has given us the privilege of being your moms.

Acknowledgements

~Loreé~

I would like to thank God for enabling me to do more than I ever dreamed possible. To my husband and best friend, Ralph, thank you for letting me follow my heart. God definitely knew what He was doing when He put us together. To Jason and Aaron, thank you for all of your help and support. You two are the best! To Josh and Cindy Wiggers, thank you for all of your help and for standing by me through the rough parts. To Denver, Alex, and all of the staff at Geography Matters, thank you for your dedication and hard work.

~Dari~

I would like to thank the Lord for His providential hand in my life. Thank You for directing my paths and leading me to places I never dreamed possible. To my husband, Allen, for loving me in spite of myself and for being the best friend and father anyone could ever have. To my best friend and sister-in-the-Lord, Loreé, thank you for always being there. You are the epitome of what God teaches us to be; I appreciate your example. I also want to thank you for taking the idea of publishing this course and running with it. I am sure you can type at least 500 wpm by now. You deserve most of the credit for this book!

We would like to extend a very special thank you to Letz Farmer of Mastery Publications for the advice and time she gave us in the development of *Galloping the Globe*. Shortly after the completion of *Galloping the Globe*, Letz was diagnosed with a rare form of cancer and passed away. Letz was a truly remarkable person that left a lasting impact on those around her. She will not be forgotten.

Galloping the Globe

Table of Contents

Instructions

Objective

The main objective of *Galloping the Globe* is to introduce students to the seven continents and a few of the countries within each continent. Along with studying geography, the students will be introduced to various historical figures, missionaries, holidays, and animals of the world. This study is geared for kindergarten to fourth grade level. It can be easily adapted to older or younger children using a few companion texts; however, the majority of the books listed under each section are for the elementary age group.

Overview

Galloping the Globe is a comprehensive unit study designed to be completed in one to three years. All subjects except math and spelling are covered. The text can also be used as a reference with any other curriculum. For more detailed information see Teaching Tips by Topic. Each section contains:

- **General Reference** – References and general information about the country or topic.

- **Geography** – Geographical terms relating to physical or topical geographic forms located in the country.

- **History and Biographies** – Missionaries, historical figures, leaders, authors, artists, musicians, scientists, and other important people who were born in or have ties with the country.

- **Literature** – Quality children's literature associated with the country, stories relating to topics studied under the country, or titles chosen just for fun and entertainment.

- **Language Arts** – Suggestions and activities to reinforce language and grammar concepts.

- **Science** – Animals, plants, and other topics that are associated with the country.

- **Bible** – Scripture references related to character traits found in the literature or pertaining to items listed in other sections of the country.

- **Activities** – A variety of crafts using readily available materials, recipes, music, and other activities pertaining to the country's culture.

- **Holidays and Celebrations** – Major holidays celebrated in the country.

- **Travel and Tourism Information** – Country travel and tourism contact information, if available, for obtaining travel brochures to use during the study.

Getting Started

Before beginning *Galloping the Globe*, please be sure your students have a globe, beginner atlas, children's dictionary, and Bible readily available. It is also helpful to have access to a set of encyclopedias, either in book form or on the computer. Most of the books used in this program were found in the authors' local library. Please check your library for these or other compatible resources before purchasing multiple books listed.

While none are mandatory, there are a few resources that you may consider buying since they are utilized throughout the duration of the course. Besides the added convenience, most of these fine books can be used for many years to come.

A note about the Core Book List: The following list has changed some since the first printing of *Galloping the Globe* when a few of the recommended resources were taken out of print. *Special Wonders of the Wild Kingdom* has been reprinted under the new title of *Magnificent Mammals* (Marvels of Creation series). *Big Book of Books and Activities* was added for use primarily with language arts as an enhancement to student notebooking.

Core Book List

- *Considering God's Creation* by Sue Mortimer and Betty Smith
- *Geography from A to Z* by Jack Knowlton
- *Our Father's World* (second grade social studies) by Rod and Staff
- *Missionary Stories with the Millers* by Mildred A. Martin
- *Great for God* (formerly *Heaven's Heroes*) by David Shibley
- *Children Just Like Me* by Barnabas and Anabel Kindersley
- *Profiles from History: Volume 1* by Ashley Wiggers
- *Big Book of Books and Activities* by Dinah Zike
- *Usborne Internet-Linked Science Encyclopedia*
- *Eat Your Way Around the World* by Jamie Aramini
- *Magnificent Mammals* by Buddy and Kay Davis or *Pocket Factfiles: Mammals* by Adam Ward Sterling
- *Zoo Guide* by Answers in Genesis
- *Aquarium Guide* by Answers in Genesis

Background Information

Before beginning *Galloping the Globe*, please familiarize yourself with the layout of the book. It is divided by continent. Within each continent, there are several countries, and within those sections there are book lists, websites, activities, ideas, etc. Look over these sections and decide which items are right for your family. Some countries do not have as many selections, as appropriate resources were not as readily available.

Books listed under each section are only suggestions. Your library or personal collection may have other wonderful resources on the subject. In most sections, there are more books suggested than necessary. With the possible exception of literature, choose one to three books per topic depending on student ability or level.

The books listed in *Galloping the Globe* have been reviewed by the authors. We tried to be extremely cautious of content, themes, and language utilized in the selections. Every family has different criteria for appropriate literature and resources. Please preview any books listed and decide if they meet your own family criteria.

As cautious as we tried to be, some of the books or websites may make reference to the earth being millions of years old or other evolutionary statements in opposition to our personal beliefs. Again, you may need to review the books before reading them to your children and use your own discernment. You may skip the evolutionary statements, change them around, or you can discuss the statements in relation to scripture. We tried not to list books that were, in our opinion, "heavy" with evolution. If we missed any, we apologize.

Creating Student Notebooks

Galloping the Globe utilizes the notebook approach at a very basic level. In this approach, the child builds a notebook throughout the length of the course, encouraging the child to be a producer rather than a consumer. This method promotes creativity and provides a permanent record of learning. The child can easily access all of his studies and share them with others. If you would like to know more about notebooking check out the following websites: www.geomatters.com, www.notebooking.org, and www.unitstudies.com.

Provide a 2″ or 3″ three-ring binder and dividers for each student. Make a divider for each continent that you study. Don't forget to include a section for Christmas Around the World.

As you study a topic, put the child's work into the appropriate section. If you wish, a separate section can be made in the notebook for Bible, providing easy access to this important character building study.

Many different items can be included in the notebook such as map work, puzzles, language arts assignments, and any other written work. When the child completes a project or activity that does not fit in the notebook, take a picture, glue it to a piece of paper, and have them write what they did under it. Use the reproducible sheets provided on the CD-ROM bound in the back of the book, for additional items to include in the child's notebook.

There are many websites listed under individual topics and on page 7. These include reproducible coloring pages, projects, maps, etc. that can be also be included in your notebooks. A fantastic resource for blank forms to be filled out and added to the notebook is *A Garden Patch of Reproducible Homeschooling Planning and Educational Worksheets* by Debora McGregor, available from Geography Matters in book form or CD-ROM.

By utilizing the notebook approach, students will have a finished book they can share with relatives and friends, reinforcing and reviewing the knowledge gained throughout the year. Students can easily refer back to their notebooks, solidifying what they have learned in addition to building confidence in themselves for the wonderful book they have created.

Galloping the Globe Activity CD-ROM

Creating the student notebook is even easier with the CD-ROM bound in the back of this book. This CD-ROM includes all of the activity sheets, maps, and flags seen in the book. You can select other bonus notebooking pages from the CD-ROM as well. This disk was added to the 2010 printing of *Galloping the Globe* so that you can conveniently print the activity sheets directly from your home computer. The disk is both Mac and PC compatible. You will need the most recent version of Adobe Reader installed on your computer to use the disk. You can download Adobe Reader for free from www.adobe.com.

Instructions

Teaching Tips by Topic

Geography

Look up these geography terms in a dictionary or *Geography from A to Z* by Jack Knowlton and use for vocabulary words. Once the child has learned several geography terms he can make a salt map of an "imaginary place" using all of the terms mastered. You'll find a salt map recipe and a fun alternative cookie dough map recipe in the Appendix.

History and Biographies

Provides a listing of specific people or historical events affiliated with the country. The historical figure, leader, author, artist, poet, or musician was born in or lived in that country. **This is not a chronological history of the world!** *Galloping the Globe* is meant to introduce some of the key people and events from different countries. It is not an exhaustive overview of world history. If your children are pre-school to fifth grade they do not need any additional history. We believe that this age should be introduced to real people who accomplished great things rather than try to learn a bunch of dates. As they get older and study specific time periods, they will remember the friends that they studied and learned about in their early years.

Literature

This section includes a wide variety of children's literature, from timeless classics to modern stories. The literature included within each country is set in the country, written by an author from the country, or relates to a topic studied in the country.

Most of the selections chosen are on an elementary reading level, or are picture books to be read aloud. Several books also include fun activities related to things which happened in the story. Encourage your children to come up with creative things to do which relate to the books they read.

Language Arts

This language arts section is **not** a complete grammar and spelling program. The activities and ideas included in this section reinforce grammar and language concepts and provide opportunities for creative writing. Choose or adapt activities to an age appropriate level for your child. A master list of language arts activities which can be used for all countries can be found on page 6. For a complete language arts course consider *Learning Language Arts Through Literature*.

Science

Science included in *Galloping the Globe* covers animals that are native to a country or are common there. In South America and Africa, science is mostly listed under the continent rather than the individual countries. In addition there is a broad spectrum of other science related topics provided throughout the course. Some of these fun topics are: trees, volcanoes, astronomy, flowers, fruits and vegetables, rain forests, deserts, and the coral reef. Internet sites that include reproducible pages, crafts, projects, and experiments are listed as well. If your child becomes interested in a specific topic, we encourage you to seek out resources and study it more in depth for as long as the child wishes.

When studying wildlife: 1) Read a book on the species. 2) In the student's notebook describe or draw a picture of the species, describe their habitat (where they live and what they eat), and tell what makes the species unique or use the Animal Report form on page 257 and on the CD-ROM. If possible, use a scripture verse that mentions the species.

Activities

This section is the "fun" stuff! There are lots of mapping activities and hands-on projects using readily available items. These activities relate to something the student is learning in that specific country. Take a picture of these activities as your children do them to add to their notebooks. Also listed are websites with various project and craft ideas, or reproducible pages on a given topic. A master list of General Activities which can be used for any country, follows this section.

Holidays and Celebrations

This section includes internet links to lists of holidays and other celebrations for that country. The websites may simply list the holidays or may contain other links with pictures, details, and other interesting information about the significant holidays for each country. The internet is a very fluid entity and therefore some of these sites may change periodically. If this does happen please go to a search engine and enter "(country name) public holidays and celebrations" for the most current websites available.

Travel and Tourism Information

Located in this section is the tourism information for each country. Contact them for brochures and information that can be utilized throughout the course. The brochures can be cut up and used in the student's notebook. The travel information can be used to discover great new places. Please allow six to eight weeks to receive the information you request.

General Activities

Select from the many interesting activities that apply to each country. Please don't try to do them all. Remember to check this list regularly as you prepare your weekly schedule.

- **Mapping Activities –** Plot the capital, major cities, rivers, mountain ranges, and other land forms on a map of the country you are studying. Maintain a world map throughout this study. Suggestions for what to include are given under each country. Geography Matters has a laminated world map that works well for this.

- **Gallop the Globe –** Lay an enlarged floor map of the world or of the continent you are studying on the floor. Use a stick horse to "gallop" from country to country. Check your local teacher supply store for a floor map or floor map puzzle.

- **Salt Map –** Draw, trace, or tape an outline of the country you are studying on a piece of cardboard. Cover with salt dough. Form mountain ranges and valleys where appropriate. Allow to dry overnight. Paint with tempura paint. A cookie dough alternative is listed in the Appendix.

- **Make a Timeline –** As you study key figures and events from each country, put their picture on a timeline on your wall, in a notebook, or both. The child can make the figure or you can use figures such as ones found on *Historical Timeline Figures CD-ROM* by Liberty Wiggers, available through Geography Matters. To help your child remember which country a person is from, have them write the country abbreviation in the corner of the timeline figure. For more information on creating a timeline notebook see the articles at www.geomatters.com.

- **Cook a Meal –** As you study each country, prepare a meal from that country. Bring the child into the kitchen with you and work on valuable life skills. Use this opportunity to discuss the diverse and unique cultures throughout the world. Some recipes are included in each section where appropriate. To prepare a complete meal typical to the countries studied in *Galloping the Globe* we recommend *Eat Your Way Around the World* by Jamie Aramini.

- **Bible –** The Bible section contains references to verses that relate to a topic studied or a character trait from literature books, or related to one of the historical figures. Use these Bible verses as memory work, copy work, or add some verses of your own and expand this section. The authors utilized the King James Version for verses. Some modern versions may use language that does not correlate with that specific topic. If this happens in your translation, refer to a King James Version for clarity.

A special "thank you" goes out to the *Galloping the Globe* discussion group which contributed some of the ideas. Come join us at: http://groups.yahoo.com/group/galloping-the-globe.

Language Arts Suggestions

- Copy Work – Have student copy word for word using their best penmanship. Use Bible verses and quotes from people you are studying or copy information about a topic you are studying. Lyrics to the national anthems can also be used. These lyrics can be found at www.national-anthems.net.

- Study simple parts of speech, such as nouns, verbs, adjectives, adverbs, article adjectives, etc. These can be pulled from books that you read. They can also be underlined in copy work. For example if you are covering verbs, have the child underline all of the verbs in that day's copy work.

- Divide sentences from reading or copy work into subject and predicate. Example: France / is located [in Europe.] "France" is the subject; "is located" is the predicate; "in Europe" is the prepositional phrase.

- Learn about the four types of sentences (declarative, interrogative, imperative, and exclamatory). Have the child identify the four types of sentences and the end mark used for each as they come across them in their reading.

- Have the child identify the four types of sentences and the end mark used for each in their own writing.

- Learn about and practice using quotation marks in reading and creative writing.

- Change a sentence from a statement to a command, question, or a direct quote and vice versa. How would this change the punctuation? How would it change the wording?

- Synonyms and antonyms – Include synonyms and antonyms when studying character traits.

- Vocabulary – Use the Dictionary page in the Appendix or a card file system. To utilize the card file system, write the root word, suffix, or prefix on the top of a 3×5 card along with its meaning. Every time you encounter a vocabulary word that has that root, suffix, or prefix, write the word and its meaning on that card and file it in a card file box. For example:

  > Astron – star
  > Astronomy – the study of stars and the atmosphere beyond the Earth

  Don't be overwhelmed by finding the root words, suffixes, and prefixes; they are easily located in a good dictionary. *F.L.A.G.S.*, listed below, also has an extensive listing of roots, suffixes, and prefixes.

- Cut a picture from a magazine of a country, animal, geographical formation, or anything else that you are studying. Glue it to a piece of colored paper. Have the child write a descriptive sentence or paragraph about the picture.

- Read or write a poem about a science topic you are studying.

- Write a report on a person, event, or science topic. We really like using the key word approach to writing reports. In this approach, the child makes a list of key words from their reading about a topic, then uses that list to retell what he has read in his own words.

- Write a play about a character trait or Bible story.

- You may want to purchase an English handbook such as *Writer's Inc.* by Great Source, to help you with grammar.

  > For more language arts ideas:
  > *Language Arts...The Easy Way* – Cindy Rushton
  > *F.L.A.G.S. (Fundamental Language Arts Game Supplemental)* – Mastery Publications
  > *A Strong Start in Language* or *The Three R's* – Ruth Beechick

6

Recommended Websites

Many fine websites can be utilized throughout the study. We've included a list here to help get you started. You might want to check back with them regularly for new additions.

- **www.groups.yahoo.com/group/galloping-the-globe/** – This is a free group that provides wonderful suggestions, web links, and activities that will enhance your study. The files section contains multiple templates for passports and other reproducible items that can be utilized throughout the entire study.

- **www.enchantedlearning.com** – This website has a multitude of useful information, including puzzles, printable books, and other items that can be used in the children's notebooks. Although this website has a paid member section, many of the items can be accessed without a membership.

- **www.national-anthems.net** – Includes links to hear the national anthems of most countries listed in *Galloping the Globe*. Also has links to see a copy of that nation's passport.

- **www.crayola.com** – Contains various coloring and activity pages to enhance your study. There are multiple helpful resources on this site. Click on the "For Educators" link to access them.

- **www.abcteach.com/directory/theme_units** – Activities and information for the children's notebooks.

- **www.birthdaycelebratons.net** – Contains information on how various countries celebrate birthdays.

- **www.aglobalworld.com/holidays-around-the-world/** – Tells how holidays are celebrated around the world. Contains lots of information about holidays, customs, and specific celebrations.

- **www.teacher.scholastic.com/mathhunt/startgame.asp?quizid=9** – This is a fun math review game that uses the holidays around the world to incorporate basic math skills. Appropriate for 3rd grade and up.

- **http://animals.nationalgeographic.com/animals** – Wonderful information, pictures and video of most of the animals in *Galloping the Globe*. Critter Cam shows animals interacting with their environments.

- **www.wildcam.com** – See live internet feeds from all over the world. Watch animals in their natural environments in real time. Also follow the action on facebook at www.facebook.com/WildCamCrittercam.

Scheduling

Every family has its own teaching and learning style. Some take a more relaxed approach while others like lots of structure. These suggestions fall somewhere in the middle. Adapt them to your family and, remember, there is no "right way" to teach this information.

- Before teaching a specific continent, decide which countries you want to study, which activities you will use, and plan what the children will include in their notebooks.

- Decide approximately how many days to spend on each country and break up the activities accordingly. Remember, the younger the child, the more varied the activities should be. Consider starting each week with an excerpt from a WeeBeeTunes DVD which uses music styles and indigenous instruments to introduce historical events, landmarks, and cultural festivals throughout the world.

- Read one to three of the literature books on the first day of each country. This will grab the children's interest and make them curious about that country.

- Locate the country on the map daily. Do other mapping activities daily with older children.

- Leave plenty of time to do some of the fun activities. Try reserving Friday for this purpose.

- Remember to be flexible! If your child shows interest in a topic or if an unexpected opportunity presents itself, adjust your schedule and go with the flow.

1

Sample Schedule for Galloping the Globe

The suggestions below are provided as a guide. There are numerous variations possible and your individual schedule will depend upon student age level and abilities. Two possible schedules are given below, feel free to use a combination of the two if desired. Please remember that *you* are in control of this curriculum and that includes the scheduling.

One country per week:
This schedule lays a foundation and gives a brief overview of the history and science topics. It is suggested this one be used for the smaller countries or when less time is available.

One country every two weeks:
This schedule allows for a more in-depth study of the country. It focuses on history from the country one week and emphasizes the science from that country the second week.

Week 1

❑ Monday
- Locate continent and country on map.
- Read some literature listed for the country.
- Do one of the activities listed.

❑ Tuesday, Wednesday, and Thursday
- Complete mapping activities and look up geography terms.
- Study and read about some of the people and events from the history and biography section.
- Do a language arts or other activity related to the history topic studied.

❑ Friday
- Review topics covered this week.
- Read about holidays and customs of the country.
- Finish any incomplete history activities or take a field trip related to your country.

Week 2

❑ Monday
- Review last week's material.
- Read some more literature from the country.
- Do one of the activities listed.

❑ Tuesday, Wednesday, and Thursday
- Fill out data box located on the map.
- Study 1–4 of the science topics listed.
- Do a language arts or other activity related to the science topic studied.

❑ Friday
- Review.
- Make sure all items are in the notebook.
- Do 1–4 of the fun activities listed.
- Prepare a meal from the country and take pictures to add to your notebook.

❑ Monday
- Locate continent and country on map.
- Read some literature listed for the country.
- Do 1–2 activities.

❑ Tuesday
- Complete some mapping activities.
- Read about a person or event from the history and biography section.
- Do a language arts activity.

❑ Wednesday
- Fill out data box located on the map and/or finish mapping activities.
- Read more literature.
- Do another activity.

❑ Thursday
- Finish or review items from map work this week.
- Read about one of the science topics.
- Do a language arts or other activity related to the science topic studied.

❑ Friday
- Review what you learned about the country.
- Place all work in your notebook.
- Do one of the fun activities listed.
- Prepare a meal from the country and take pictures to add to your notebook.

Instructions

Adapting to Older Students

Galloping the Globe can be adapted to older students quite easily. By using a few extra texts, an older student can gain a very in-depth, thorough knowledge of our world. The recommended resources below are available from Geography Matters:

- *Trail Guide to World Geography* by Cindy Wiggers – This guide can be used as the child's primary text. Use the suggestions and format provided to give the older student a solid foundation of world geography. Utilize the research ideas listed under each country to include other subjects such as language arts and the arts.

- *A Garden Patch of Reproducible Homeschooling Planning and Educational Worksheets* by Debora McGregor – This has a variety of report forms, interview sheets, and research sheets that the older student can use in their notebooks.

- *All Through the Ages* by Christine Miller – This is a great book that lists literature for various time periods and countries. The author breaks the lists up by genre, such as historical fiction, reference, etc., and by age level. It is a fantastic resource to utilize when needing additional resources for children of any age.

Resource Contact Information

The following companies carry many of the titles recommended throughout this curriculum. The contact information is provided for your convenience and was accurate at the time of publication:

Book Peddler
800-928-1760
www.bookpeddler.us

- Books by Opal Wheeler recommended for Germany
- *Your Story Hour* audios
- *Classical Kids* audios

Dinah Might Adventures
800-993-4624
www.dinah.com

- *Big Book of Books and Activities*

Geography Matters
800-426-4650
www.geomatters.com

- *Considering God's Creation*
- *Geography from A to Z*
- *Missionary Stories with the Millers*
- *Great for God* (Heaven's Heroes)
- *Children Just Like Me*
- *Profiles from History: Volume 1*
- *All Through The Ages*
- Historical Timeline Figures
- *Eat Your Way Around the World*
- *Magnificent Mammals*
- *Beginner or Jr. World Atlas*
- WeeBeeTunes DVDs
- *Trail Guide to World Geography*
- *Garden Patch of Reproducibles*
- *Zoo Guide*
- *Aquarium Guide*

Rod and Staff
606-522-4348
www.rodandstaffbooks.com

- *Our Father's World* (Code:19221)

Solomon's Secrets
www.solomons-secrets.com

- Usborne books
- Jim Weiss audios

Timberdoodle
800-478-0672
www.timberdoodle.com

- *Ten Boys* series and *Ten Girls* series (Irene Horvat)
- Moody Science Videos

Instructions

The World

Home to almost 7 billion people in over 190 countries, the world is most often divided into seven major land regions called continents. Made up of approximately 70% water and 30% land, the overall size of the world is about sixteen times the size of the United States. The continent of Asia has both the highest and lowest points in the world. The highest point on earth is 29,035 ft. at Mount Everest in the Himalayan Mountains. The lowest point is the Dead Sea (-1349 ft.) in Israel.

The World

Color each continent you study.

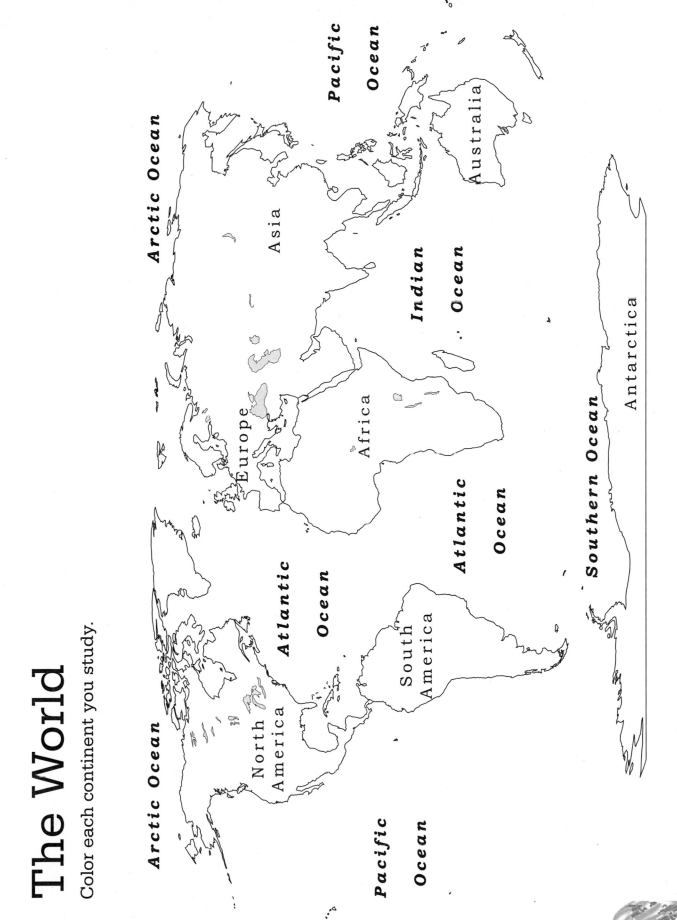

Arctic Ocean

Pacific Ocean

Atlantic Ocean

North America

South America

Pacific Ocean

Europe

Africa

Asia

Indian Ocean

Atlantic Ocean

Australia

Southern Ocean

Antarctica

Arctic Ocean

The World

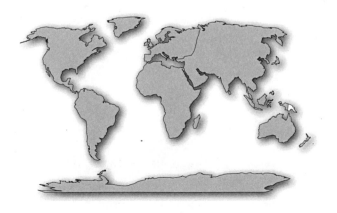

Using a Map

Begin this unit by covering basic map and globe skills.

- ❑ *Maps and Globes* – Jack Knowlton
- ❑ *Maps and Mapping* – Barbara Taylor
- ❑ *How to Use a Map* – Evan-Moor Publishers
- ❑ *Globes* (A New True Book) – Paul P. Sipiera
- ❑ *Our Father's World,* pages 41–42
- ❑ *Our Father's World,* pages 46–48
- ❑ *Our Father's World,* pages 96–98

Children should know north, south, east, and west and the difference between land and water. *Katy and the Big Snow* by Virginia Lee Burton is an excellent children's book to introduce them to direction.

Notebook Suggestions:

- ❑ *How to Use a Map* – Evan-Moor Publishers
- ❑ Make a map of your house, neighborhood, or a park.

Basic Geography

Geography – A description of the earth or globe.

Christian geography is the view that the earth's origins, ends, and purposes are of Christ and for His glory.

- ❑ Continents
  - *Geography from A to Z,* page 13
  - *Continents* (A New True Book)* – Dennis B. Fradin (Note: evolutionary content)
  - *Our Father's World,* pages 37–40
- ❑ Oceans
  - *Geography from A to Z,* page 32
  - *The Pacific Ocean* (A New True Book)* – Susan Heinrichs
  - *The Atlantic Ocean* (A New True Book)* – Susan Heinrichs
  - *The Indian Ocean* (A New True Book)* – Susan Heinrichs
  - *Our Father's World,* pages 43–45

*These books can be a bit lengthy to hold a young elementary student's attention. We recommend just covering the highlights.

History and Biographies

- ❑ Mercator
  - www.yesnet.yk.ca/schools/projects/renaissance/mercator.html
- ❑ Prince Henry the Navigator
  - www.enchantedlearning.com/explorers/page/h/henry.shtml
  - www.mrdowling.com/610-henry.html
- ❑ Bartholomew Diaz
- ❑ Explorers
  - *The Usborne Book of Explorers,* page 3
  - *Explorers* (A New True Book)
  - *Explorers and Adventurers* – Child's First Library of Learning
- ❑ Christopher Columbus
  - *The Usborne Book of Explorers,* page 22
  - www.enchantedlearning.com/explorers/page/c/columbus.shtml
  - http://library.thinkquest.org/J002678F/columbus.htm
  - *Christopher Columbus* – Stephen Krensky – Step into Reading
  - *Christopher Columbus* – Tanya Larkin
  - *Christopher Columbus* – Young Christian Library
  - *Follow the Dream* – Peter Sis
  - *Columbus* – D'Aulaire
  - *Christopher Columbus* – Animated Hero Classics Video
- ❑ Francis Drake
  - *The Usborne Book of Explorers,* page 39
  - *Sir Francis Drake* – Tanya Larkin
  - *Francis Drake* – David Goodnough
  - www.enchantedlearning.com/explorers/page/d/drake.shtml
- ❑ Cabeza de Vaca
  - www.enchantedlearning.com/explorers/page/d/devaca.shtml
  - *Cabeza de Vaca: New World Explorer* – Keith Brandt
- ❑ Vasco da Gama
  - *Vasco da Gama* – Tanya Larkin
  - *The Usborne Book of Explorers,* page 18
- ❑ John Cabot
  - www.enchantedlearning.com/explorers/page/c/cabot.shtml
- ❑ Amerigo Vespucci
  - *Around the World in a Hundred Years* – Jean Fritz
- ❑ Juan Ponce de Leon
  - *Juan Ponce de Leon* – Gail Sakurai
  - www.enchantedlearning.com/explorers/page/d/deleon.shtml

- ❑ Vasco Núñez de Balboa
  - *Around the World in a Hundred Years* – Jean Fritz
  - www.enchantedlearning.com/explorers/page/b/balboa.shtml
- ❑ Ferdinand Magellan
  - *Around the World in a Hundred Years* – Jean Fritz
  - www.enchantedlearning.com/explorers/page/m/magellan.shtml
- ❑ Hernando de Soto
  - *Hernando de Soto* – Tanya Larkin

General References

- ❑ *Our Father's World,* pages 100–113

Literature

- ❑ *Toot and Puddle* – Holly Hobbie
- ❑ *How To Make An Apple Pie and See the World* – Marjorie Priceman
- ❑ *Miss Rumphius* – Barbara Cooney
- ❑ *Katy and the Big Snow* – Virginia Lee Burton
- ❑ *Amelia's Fantastic Flight* – Rose Bursik
- ❑ *Letters from Felix* – Annette Langen (An activity book is also available.)

Language Arts

- ❑ Choose from the Language Arts Suggestions on page 6.
- ❑ Make a list of adjectives describing insects.
- ❑ Alphabetize the explorer's names.

Science

God has a purpose for the Earth. The Earth is part of the universe and one of nine known planets that circle the sun.

- ❑ *Considering God's Creation,* lesson 2
- ❑ Insects
  - www.enchantedlearning.com/themes/insects.shtml
  - www.crayola.com/activitybook/subact.cfm?id=76&maincat=4
  - www.coloring.ws/insect.htm
  - www.urbanext.illinois.edu/insects/
  - http://kids.nationalgeographic.com/Animals/CreatureFeature
  - *God made the Firefly,* God is Good Series published by Rod and Staff
  - *Creepy Crawlies* – Wendy Madgwick
  - *Bugs for Lunch* – Margery Facklam
  - *Monster Bugs* – Lucille Recht Penner
  - *Insects* – Golden Book (ISBN: 0-307-20400-6)
  - *Little Honeybee* – Baby Animal Stories (ISBN: 0-7853-2680-4)
  - *Honey Bees and Hives* – Lola M. Schaefer
  - *Bumble Bees* – Cheryl Coughlan
  - *Fireflies* – Cheryl Coughlan
  - *Mosquitoes* – Cheryl Coughlan

- *Ladybugs* – Cheryl Coughlan
- *Pets in a Jar* – Seymour Simon
- *The Very Quiet Cricket* – Eric Carle
- *The Very Lonely Firefly* – Eric Carle
- *The Icky Bug Counting Book* – Jerry Pallotta
- *Bugs! Bugs! Bugs!* – Bob Barner
- *Considering God's Creation*, lesson 13

❑ Butterflies
- *Butterflies* – Emily Neye
- *Butterflies and Moths,* Usborne First Nature
- *Amazing World of Butterflies and Moths* – Louis Sabin (Except for evolutionary statements on page 5, this a wonderful book. If you choose to read it, just skip page 5.)
- *Monarch Butterflies* – Helen Frost
- *Butterfly Colors* – Helen Frost
- www.enchantedlearning.com/themes/butterfly.shtml
- www.primarygames.com/science/butterflies/coloring.htm
- www.coloring.ws/butterfly1.htm

Activities

❑ Make a papier mâche earth.

❑ Label the Arctic, Atlantic, Pacific, and Indian Oceans on a world map.

❑ If you read *How to Make an Apple Pie and See the World*, bake an apple pie.

❑ If you studied insects, make ice cream ants.

vanilla ice cream	Magic Shell chocolate coating
pretzel sticks	M&M's®
shoe string licorice	

On a plate, place three small scoops of ice cream in a line.

Place two M&Ms® on the "head" for the eyes. Cut an M&M® in half. Use the two halves as the mouth. Use the licorice as the antennae.

Poke three pretzel sticks per side in the middle section or "thorax."

Cover the whole "ant" with Magic Shell as the "exoskeleton."

❑ Have the child write a creative story of himself/herself as an explorer.

❑ Have the child draw a picture of an explorer or of himself/herself as an explorer.

❑ Make an ant colony.

❑ Play the "Bug Game" by Ampersand Press.

❑ Catch butterflies or make a butterfly habitat. Butterfly Jungle by Uncle Milton provides the habitat and includes a coupon that you use to order live caterpillars. Include a picture or report of this project in your notebook.

Bible

- ❑ *How to Make an Apple Pie and See the World*
  - Genesis 1:1
  - Psalm 113:4
  - Proverbs 25:11

- ❑ *Katy and the Big Snow*
  - Genesis 39:19–41:13
  - I Peter 5:6

- ❑ *Miss Rumphius*
  - Genesis 8:22
  - Matthew 13:1–8
  - Matthew 13:31–32
  - Mark 4:3–8
  - Mark 4:26–29
  - Mark 4:30–32
  - Luke 8:4–8
  - Luke 13:18–19
  - John 1:1,3,14
  - 2 Corinthians 9:10
  - Galatians 6:7

- ❑ God is responsible for the contour of the Earth.
  - Genesis 1:1–8
  - Nehemiah 9:6
  - Job 28:9–11
  - Job 26:7–12
  - Isaiah 40:22
  - Isaiah 48:13

- ❑ God controls His creation.
  - Genesis 1:9–25
  - Job 36:26–28
  - Psalm 24:1
  - Psalm 107:23–31
  - Psalm 113:4

- ❑ God originated nations and languages.
  - Genesis 10:5
  - Genesis 11:1–9
  - Job 12:23
  - Isaiah 45:18
  - Acts 17:24–28

- ❑ God is concerned with all people.
  - Matthew 28:19
  - John 4
  - Acts 1:8
  - Acts 2:5–11
  - Acts 10:34
  - Romans 10:12, 13

Continents

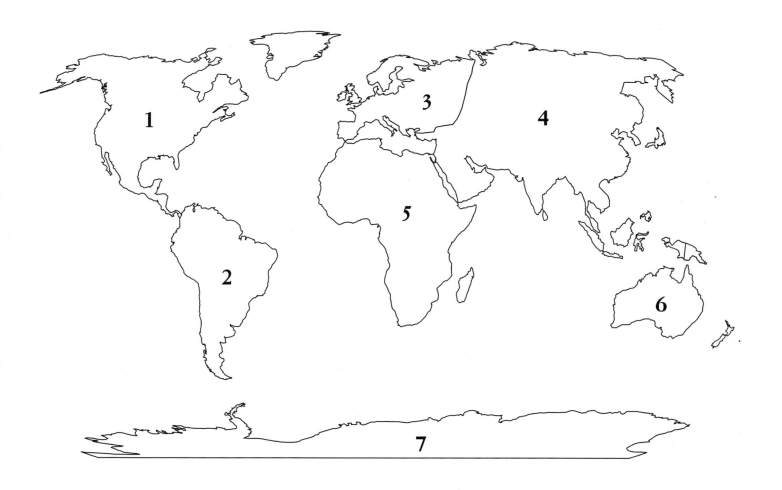

1. _____

2. _____

3. _____

4. _____

5. _____

6. _____

7. _____

Word List

Africa
Asia
Oceania (Australia)
Europe
North America
South America
Antarctica

Word Search

```
v u g j i c i g l o b e
e a s t y o b e t y l k
i u g u l l s x i i f t
m c b i f u m p i n t a
a t c n l m l l r a s p
p t v o f b e o m e j c
p b d r n u a r f n i o
w e s t o s s e h z d m
s y z h f n f r q s x p
s o u t h d c y u l j a
n d q k o c e a n n d s
n i n a s i q m r b q s
```

Columbus
compass
east
explorer
globe
map

Nina
north
ocean
Pinta
south
west

Word Search

```
q  p  c  o  n  t  i  n  e  n  t  g
q  a  s  i  a  z  z  a  x  f  s  x
r  f  h  o  r  x  j  n  o  r  t  h
s  r  z  k  x  k  b  t  r  f  s  z
r  i  b  m  k  k  p  a  z  r  s  v
z  c  x  w  v  z  x  r  h  x  o  e
c  a  j  l  e  u  k  c  j  d  u  e
n  o  x  p  u  q  u  t  a  l  t  w
a  u  s  t  r  a  l  i  a  s  h  w
s  a  t  y  o  m  b  c  a  m  s  e
f  l  u  y  p  x  j  a  c  a  c  e
h  h  a  m  e  r  i  c  a  j  l  h
```

Africa
America
Antarctica
Asia
Australia

Continent
Europe
North
South

The World

MAZE CRAZE

The World

connect the dots

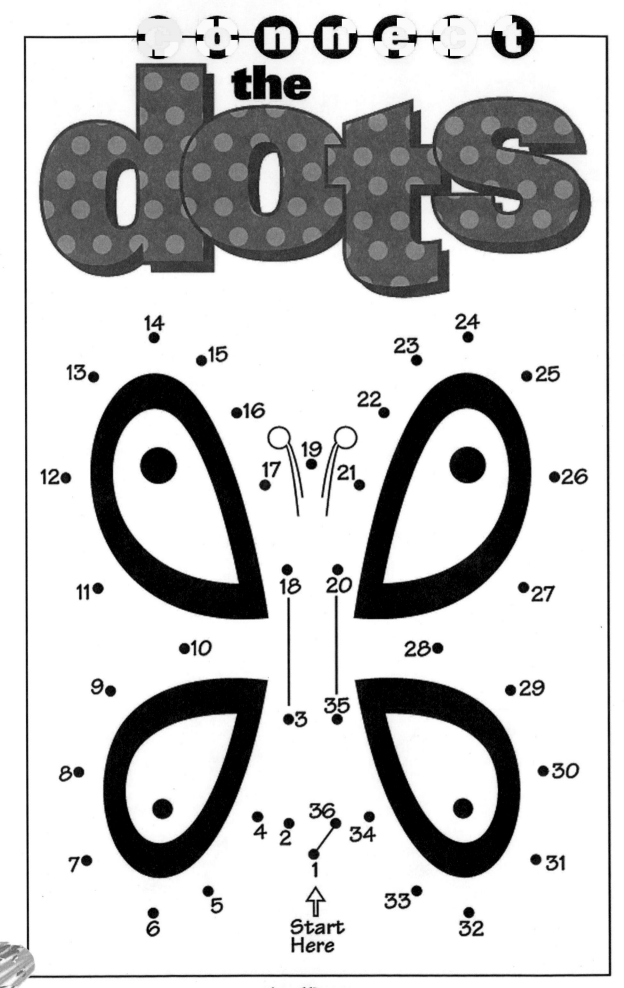

Start Here

The World

Asia

Asia is the largest continent in the world and home to over 3.7 billion people. Its two most populated countries are China and India. The highest point in Asia is 29,028 feet at Mt. Everest in China, between Nepal and Tibet. The lowest elevation is at the Dead Sea in Israel, Jordan, where it is 1,339 feet below sea level. Asia is separated from Europe by the Ural Mountains.

Asia

Color each country you study.

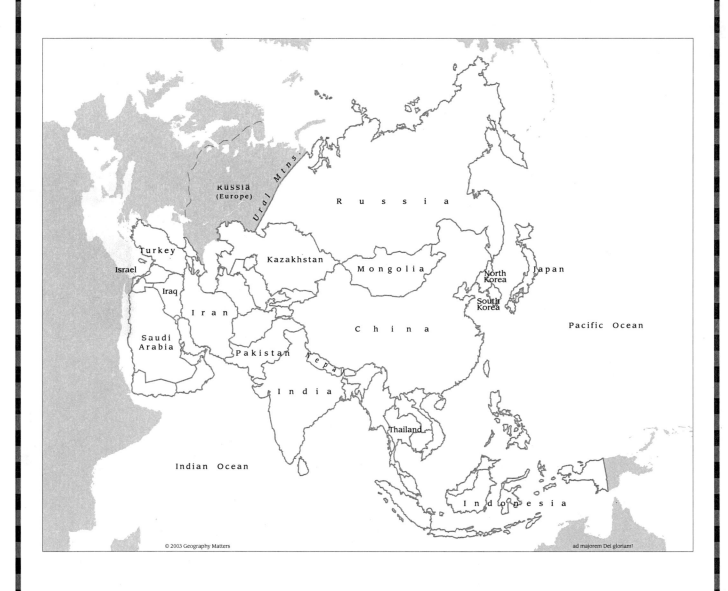

Turkey
Israel
Iraq
Iran
Saudi Arabia
Russia (Europe)
Ural Mtns.
Russia
Kazakhstan
Mongolia
North Korea
South Korea
Japan
China
Pacific Ocean
Pakistan
Nepal
India
Thailand
Indian Ocean
Indonesia

© 2003 Geography Matters

ad majorem Dei gloriam!

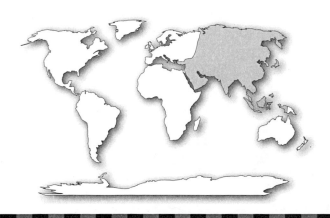

Asia

China

Population _____

Capital City _____

Religion _____

Type of Government _____

Currency _____

Language _____

What are the people called? _____

26

China

China

Home to one-fifth of the world's population, China is the world's third largest country. It also has the oldest continual civilization. The ancient Chinese thought that their country was the center of the world and that they were the only truly civilized people. They called their country Chung-kuo, which means "middle country." The capital of China is Beijing.

The Chinese flag, five gold stars on a red field, was adopted in 1949. Five is an important number in Chinese philosophy. The large star represents the Communist Party and the four smaller stars symbolize the classes in Chinese society. Red is a traditional Chinese color.

Covering most of eastern Asia, China is a vast land of majestic mountains, dry deserts, grassy plains, and fertile farmland. Two of the longest rivers in China, the Huang He, or Yellow River, and the Yangtze, are also two of the longest rivers in the world.

Geography

❑ Yangtze River

❑ River
- *Geography from A to Z,* page 38
- *Usborne Internet-Linked Science Encyclopedia,* pages 190–191

History and Biographies

❑ Hudson Taylor
- *Hudson Taylor* – Young Christian Library
- *Missionary Stories with the Millers* – "Too Busy Fishing," chapter 8

❑ Eric Liddell
- *Eric Liddell* – Young Christian Library
- *Great for God (Heaven's Heroes)* – "Flying Scot," chapter 9
- *Ten Boys Who Changed the World* – Irene Howat, pages 47–59

❑ Marco Polo
- *Marco Polo* – Gian Paolo Ceserani
- www.enchantedlearning.com/explorers/page/p/polo.shtml
- *Profiles from History,* page 11

❑ Lottie Moon
- *Ten Girls Who Made History* – Irene Howat, page 49 (available from Timberdoodle)
- www.historyswomen.com/womenoffaith/lottiemoon.html

- ❑ Qin Shi Huangdi
  - *Qin Shi Huangdi: First Emperor of China* – Peggy Pencella
- ❑ Terra Cotta Army
  - www.hbschool.com/newsbreak/terra.html
- ❑ Great Wall of China
  - *The Great Wall of China* – Leonard Everett Fisher

General References

- ❑ *Chasing the Moon to China* – Virginia Overton McLean
- ❑ *Count Your Way Through China* – Jim Haskins
- ❑ *Country Insights: China* – Julia Waterlow
- ❑ *Wonders of China* – Lynn M. Stone
- ❑ *The Provinces and Cities of China* – Lynn M. Stone
- ❑ *A Family in China* – Nance Lui Fyson
- ❑ *A Family in Hong Kong* – Peter Otto Jacobsen
- ❑ *Children Just Like Me,* pages 48–49
- ❑ *China, Here We Come!* – Tang Yungmei
- ❑ *China* – Michael Dahl
- ❑ *China* – Ann Heinrichs
- ❑ *Letters from Around the World: China* – Julia Waterlow

Literature

- ❑ *Missionary Stories with the Millers,* chapter 3
- ❑ *Story About Ping* – Marjorie Flack
- ❑ *Stories From Around the World:* "Ivory Wand" (Usborne)
- ❑ "Secret Weapon" from *Tales from Cultures Far and Near,* audio by Jim Weiss
- ❑ *Granny Han's Breakfast* – Sheila Groves
- ❑ *Little Pear* – Eleanor Frances Lattimore
- ❑ *A Little Tiger in the Chinese Night* – Song Nan Zhang
- ❑ *Tikki Tikki Tembo* – Arlene Mosel
- ❑ *The Chinese Mirror* – M. Ginsburg
- ❑ *Li Lun, Lad of Courage* – Carolyn Treffinge
- ❑ *In the Sun* – Huy Voun Lee
- ❑ *In the Snow* – Huy Voun Lee
- ❑ *In the Park* – Huy Voun Lee
- ❑ *At the Beach* – Huy Voun Lee
- ❑ *The Empty Pot* – Demi
- ❑ *The Greatest Treasure* – Demi

Language Arts

❑ Choose from the Language Arts Suggestions on page 6.

❑ Make a desk-top project book of the Great Wall of China. Refer to the *Big Book of Books and Activities*, page 42.

Science

❑ Duck
  • *A Duckling is Born* – Hans-Heinrich Isenbart
  • *Ducks Don't Get Wet* – Augusta Goldin
  • *Aquarium Guide*, page 191
  • www.enchantedlearning.com/themes/duck.shtml

❑ Panda
  • *Magnificent Mammals*, page 28
  • *Giant Pandas* – Marcia S. Freeman
  • *Wild Bears! Panda* – Tom and Pat Leeson
  • *Zoo Guide*, page 43
  • www.enchantedlearning.com/subjects/mammals/panda/
  • www.zooatlanta.org/home/animals/mammals/giant_panda
  • www.zooatlanta.org/home/animals/mammals/red_panda
  • http://kids.nationalgeographic.com/Animals/CreatureFeature/Panda
  • http://video.nationalgeographic.com/video/player/animals/mammals-animals/bears-and-pandas/bear_brown_crittercam.html

❑ Sloth Bears
  • http://animals.nationalgeographic.com/animals/mammals/sloth-bear.html

❑ Snow Leopard
  • *Pocket Factfiles: Mammals,* pages 16–17
  • http://animals.nationalgeographic.com/animals/mammals/snow-leopard.html

Activities

❑ Color or make the flag of China. Use gold foil stars on red paper. Add it to your notebook.

❑ Color or label a map of China.

❑ Label the Yangtze River on a world map.

❑ Make a Chinese meal from *Eat Your Way Around the World*.

❑ Go to www.enchantedlearning.com/themes/china.shtml for information, printable activities, and craft ideas.

❑ Read *Dover Coloring Book Chinese Fashions* by Ming-Ju Sun.

❑ Play ping-pong, China's national sport.

❑ Go to www.crayola.com/activitybook/print.cfm?id=898 for a Chinese lantern craft.

Bible

- ❑ *The Empty Pot*
  - Proverbs 12:22
  - 2 Corinthians 8:21
  - Ephesians 4:25
  - Colossians 3:9

- ❑ *Missionary Stories with the Millers*, chapter 8
  - Matthew 4:19

- ❑ Great Wall of China
  - Genesis 11:1–9

- ❑ *Story About Ping*
  - I Peter 2:13–20

- ❑ Leopard
  - Isaiah 11:6

Holidays and Celebrations

- ❑ *Chinese New Year* – Alice K. Flanagan
- ❑ *Chinese New Year* – Judith Jango-Cohen
- ❑ *My First Chinese New Year* – Karen Katz
- ❑ www.educ.uvic.ca/faculty/mroth/438/CHINA/chinese_new_year.html
- ❑ http://en.wikipedia.org/wiki/Holidays_in_the_People%27s_Republic_of_China
- ❑ www.index-china.com/index-english/chinese_holidays.htm
- ❑ www.chinavoc.com/festivals/index.asp
- ❑ www.gio.gov.tw/info/festival_c/glue_e/glue.htm
- ❑ www.ncsu.edu/midlink/dec97/holiday/boatz.html

Travel and Tourism

China National Tourist Office
350 Fifth Ave, Suite 6413
New York, NY 10118

Telephone: 212-760-9700

Email: cntony@aol.com

Website: www.cnto.org

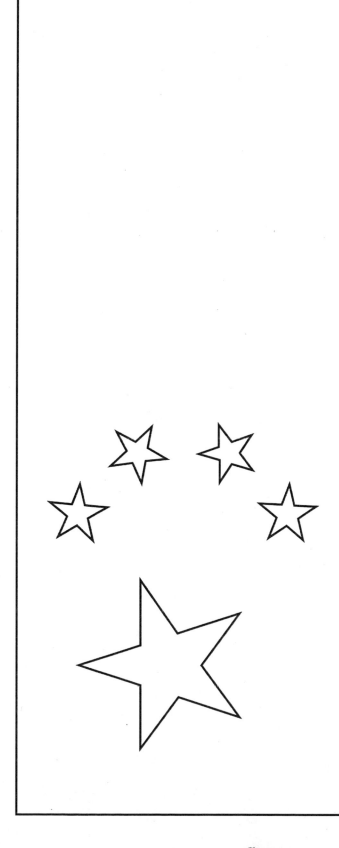

Flag of China

China

South Korea

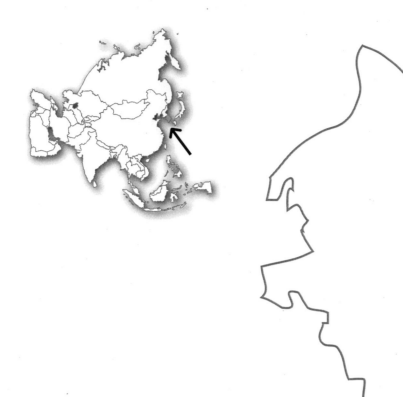

Population _____

Capital City _____

Religion _____

Type of Government _____

Currency _____

Language _____

What are the people called? _____

32

South Korea

At the end of World War II, the Korean Peninsula was divided at the 38th parallel. The Republic of Korea, or South Korea as it is commonly referred to, is on the southern half of the peninsula. It is about the size of the state of Utah. South Korea is known as the "Land of the Morning Calm," and its capital is Seoul.

The South Korean flag is a red and blue yin yang symbol surrounded by trigrams of black bars on four sides, all on a field of white. Red, white, and blue are traditional Korean colors. The yin yang symbolizes balance and harmony between opposites. The unbroken bars on the upper left represent heaven. The bars on the upper right stand for water. The bars on the lower left signify fire. The broken bars on the lower right represent Earth.

Prior to World War II, when Japan controlled the peninsula, North and South Korea were one nation. When Japan was defeated, the peninsula was divided in two. Communists gained control of North Korea and are still in power today. South Korea has remained strongly anti-Communist.

In 1950, the Korean War began when North Korea invaded South Korea. After three years of fighting, neither side had won a decisive victory. A permanent peace treaty was never signed and the war has never officially ended.

History and Biography
❑ Bob Pierce
   • *Great for God (Heaven's Heroes)*, chapter 14
   • *Missionary Stories with the Millers,* chapter 18

General References
❑ *Take a Trip to South Korea* – Keith Lye

❑ *Next Stop South Korea* – Fred Martin

❑ *Count Your Way Through Korea* – Jim Haskins

❑ *A Family in South Korea* – Gwynneth Ashby

❑ *Children of the World: South Korea* – Makoto Kubota

❑ *Children Just Like Me,* pages 54–55

❑ *South Korea* – Lucille Davis

❑ www.lifeinkorea.com/pictures/

Literature
❑ *The Green Frogs* – Yumi Heo

Language Arts

❑ Choose from the Language Arts Suggestions on page 6.

❑ The flag of South Korea uses yin and yang – opposites. Use this time to discuss antonyms with your child. See how many they can think of and have them draw their ideas on a divided sheet of paper. Or make a vocabulary book. Refer to the *Big Book of Books and Activities,* page 21.

Science

❑ *Considering God's Creation,* lesson 15

❑ *The Wonders of God's Creation: Animal Kingdom* – Moody Institute of Science Video

Activities

❑ Color or make the flag of Korea.

❑ Color or label a map of Korea.

❑ Label the Yellow Sea on a world map.

❑ Make Korean Barbecued Beef.

1 lb. Sirloin steak	¼ cup soy sauce	3 tablespoons sugar
2 tablespoons oil	¼ teaspoon pepper	2 cloves garlic, chopped
3 green onions, finely chopped		

Directions: Trim fat. Cut beef across the grain in ⅛-inch strips. Mix remaining ingredients; stir in beef until well coated. Refrigerate 30 minutes. Drain beef; stir fry in skillet or wok over medium heat until light brown. Serve with hot cooked rice.

❑ Make a Korean meal from *Eat Your Way Around the World.*

❑ Play "rock, scissors, paper." It originated in Korea where it is called "kawi, bawi, bo."

Bible

❑ *Missionary Stories with the Millers,* chapter 18
  • 1 Kings 17:1
  • James 5:17

❑ *The Green Frogs*
  • Ephesians 6:1
  • Isaiah 1:19
  • Hebrews 13:17
  • Colossians 3:20

Holidays and Celebrations

❑ http://en.wikipedia.org/wiki/Public_holidays_in_South_Korea

❑ www.asia-pacific-connections.com/korean_holidays.html

❑ www.clickasia.co.kr/about/h815.htm

❑ www.clickasia.co.kr/about/h0101.htm

Travel and Tourism

Korea National Tourism Organization
4801 Wilshire Blvd., Ste. 103
Los Angeles, CA 90010

Telephone: 1-800-868-7567 (toll-free in USA)
Telephone: 323-643-0025
Email: kntola@mail.wcis.com

Flag of South Korea

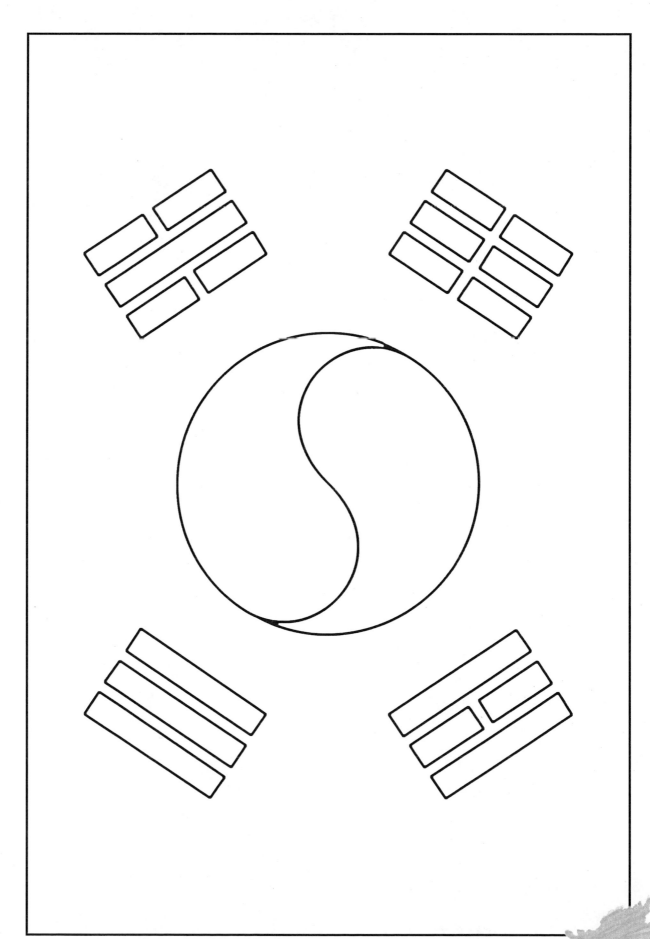

South Korea

Japan

Population _____

Capital City _____

Religion _____

Type of Government _____

Currency _____

Language _____

What are the people called? _____

Japan

Japan

Made up of four large islands and thousands of smaller ones, Japan stretches across 1,200 miles in the Northern Pacific Ocean. If you combined all of the land area of the islands, Japan would be a little smaller than the state of California. The Japanese call their country "Nippon," which means "Land of the Rising Sun." Tokyo is the capital of Japan.

Adopted in 1870, the flag of Japan is a red circle on a white field. The circle symbolizes the sun and has been part of Japan's national flag for centuries.

Long isolated from the world, Japan began to modernize in the 1870's. This modernization began after Commodore Matthew Perry established a trade agreement with Japan in 1854. Today, Japan is one of the most industrialized countries in the world and a leader in technology.

Geography
- ❑ Archipelago
  - *Geography from A to Z,* page 7

History and Biographies
- ❑ Hokusai
  - *Hokusai* – Deborah Kogan Ray
- ❑ Commodore Matthew C. Perry
- ❑ Emperor Hirohito

General References
- ❑ *A Visit to Japan* – Peter and Connie Roop
- ❑ *A Family in Japan* – Peter Otto Jacobsen
- ❑ *Japan* (A True Book) – Ann Heinrichs
- ❑ *Count Your Way Though Japan* – Jim Haskins
- ❑ *Look What Came From Japan* – Miles Harvey
- ❑ *Japan* – Tamara L. Britton
- ❑ *Next Stop Japan* – Clare Boast
- ❑ *Japan* – Susan Sinnot
- ❑ *We Come from Japan* – Teresa Fisher
- ❑ *Children Just Like Me,* pages 52–53

Literature
- ❑ *Grandfather's Journey* – Allen Say

- ❑ *A Carp for Kimiko* – Virginia Kroll
- ❑ *The Bicycle Man* – Allen Say
- ❑ *The Wise Old Woman* – Yoshiko Uchida
- ❑ *The Two Foolish Cats* – Yoshiko Uchida
- ❑ *The Rooster Who Understood Japanese* – Yoshiko Uchida
- ❑ *How My Parents Learned to Eat* – Ina Friedman
- ❑ *Crow Boy* – Taro Yashima
- ❑ *Japanese Children's Favorite Stories* – Florence Sakade
- ❑ "Two Monks" from *Tales from Cultures Far and Near,* audio by Jim Weiss
- ❑ *Suki's Kimono* – Chieri Uegaki
- ❑ *Yoshi's Feast* – Kimiko Kajikawa
- ❑ *The Boy of the Three-Year Nap* – Dianne Snyder
- ❑ *Pair of Red Clogs* – Masako Matsuno

Language Arts

- ❑ Choose from the Language Arts Suggestions on page 6.
- ❑ The Japanese have a special holiday honoring the aged members in their society and recognizing the contributions they have made. Have your child write a letter to a grandparent or other aged relative thanking them for their specific contribution to our society or your family.

Science

- ❑ *Considering God's Creation*, lesson 19
- ❑ Japanese Macaque
    - www.blueplanetbiomes.org/japanese_macaque.htm

Activities

- ❑ Color or make the flag of Japan.

    Trace a CD on a plain piece of paper and let the child color it. Or, trace a CD on a piece of red paper, let the child cut out the circle and glue it on a piece of plain paper.

- ❑ Color or label a map of Japan.
- ❑ Label the Sea of Japan on a world map.
- ❑ Make Origami.

    Check your local library for books on origami. Craft and teacher supply stores have brightly colored paper perfect for origami.

- ❑ Play Karuta.

    Poetry is so much a part of everyday life in Japan that a card game called Karuta, or "One Hundred Poems," is very popular.

    - Copy half of popular or familiar poems onto two index cards. First half on one card; second half on second card. Keep the first half in a separate stack.
    - Choose a leader to read the opening half of a well-known poem from a card; whoever matches the card with the other half of the poem (among the many spread out on the table) gets to keep it.
    - The player with the most cards at the end of the game is the winner.

❑ Have a crab race.

To play this game, have the children rise up on all fours with their back facing the floor. Have them "race" to the finish line.

❑ Make a Japanese meal from *Eat Your Way Around the World*.

❑ If your budget allows, go to a Japanese restaurant that cooks hibachi style, where the chef chops and cooks the food at your table.

❑ Go to www.crayola.com/activitybook/print.cfm?id=897 for a Japanese lantern craft.

❑ Go to www.dltk-kids.com/world/japan/posters/ for printable coloring pages.

Bible

❑ *Grandfather's Journey*
  • Psalm 34:18
  • Psalm 137:1–5
  • Matthew 7:12
  • 2 Corinthians 1:3–4
  • James 3:18

❑ *The Wise Old Woman*
  • Proverbs 8:12
  • Proverbs 10:14
  • Proverbs 12:15
  • Proverbs 17:24
  • Luke 18:14
  • Romans 12:3
  • Philippians 2:3
  • I Peter 5:5

❑ *Two Foolish Cats*
  • Proverbs 3:35
  • Proverbs 14:21
  • Ecclesiastes 7:9
  • Matthew 5:42
  • Acts 20:35
  • Philippians 2:4, 20–21

❑ *The Rooster Who Understood Japanese*
  • Proverbs 11:13
  • Proverbs 13:20
  • Proverbs 19:15
  • Proverbs 25:20–21
  • Luke 6:35

Holidays and Celebrations

❑ www.embjapan.dk/culture/default.htm

❑ www.japan-guide.com/e/e2062.html

❑ www.geocities.com/Tokyo/Ginza/8930/Izu/

❑ www.familyculture.com/holidays/japanese_new_year.htm

Travel and Tourism

Japan National Tourist Organization
One Rockefeller Plaza, Suite 1250
New York, NY 10020

Telephone: 212-757-5640

Email: info@jntonyc.org

Website: www.japantravelinfo.com

39

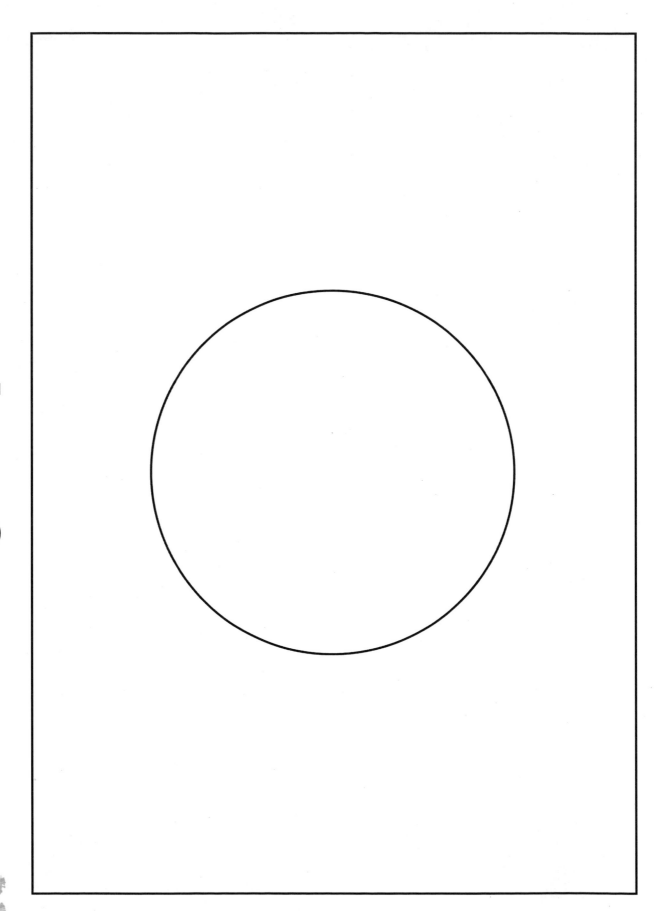

Flag of Japan

Japan

Japan

India

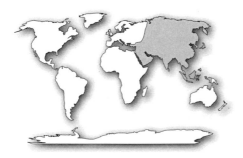

Population _____

Capital City _____

Religion _____

Type of Government _____

Currency _____

Language _____

What are the people called? _____

India

42

India

Home to a population second only to China, India is the largest country in southern Asia. Bordered by the Himalaya Mountains to the north and the Indian Ocean to the west, south, and east, India is an ancient land of diverse ethnic groups and varying landscapes. Once a land of mystery and wealth, India's natural resources were not developed causing great poverty. The overcrowded cities have very poor living conditions among the lower castes. The capital of India is New Delhi.

India's flag is vertical stripes of orange, white, and green with an ancient symbol called the "Dharma Chakra" in the center. The Chakra is also called the "Wheel of the Law." The twenty-four spokes of the wheel represent the twenty-four hours in a day. The orange stripe stands for courage and sacrifice. White is for peace and truth. Green symbolizes faith. The flag was adopted in 1947.

Although Buddhism, Jainism, and Sikhism also began in India, eighty percent of all Indians are practicing Hindus. Hindus worship many gods. Hinduism divides people into castes that determine how well a person lives and the type of job they can have. Hinduism teaches that souls are reborn many times, that animals have souls, and that cows are sacred.

Geography
❑ Sea
  • *Geography from A to Z,* page 39

History and Biographies
❑ Amy Carmichael
  • *Missionary Stories with the Millers,* chapter 20
  • *Ten Girls Who Changed the World* – Irene Howat, pages 39–51

❑ William Carey
  • *Missionary Stories with the Millers,* chapter 23
  • *The Shoemaker Who Pioneered Modern Missions* – Ben Alex
  • *Ten Boys Who Changed the World* – Irene Howat, pages 61–73

❑ Gandhi
  • *What's Their Story?: Gandhi* – Pratima Mitchell
  • *Gandhi: Peaceful Warrior* – Rae Bains

General References
❑ *India* – David Cumming

❑ *India* – Michael Dahl

❑ *A Family in India* – Tony Tigwell

❑ *Our Father's World,* pages 62–68

❑ *Children Just Like Me,* pages 56–59

Literature

❑ *Missionary Stories with the Millers,* chapter 13

❑ *Missionary Stories with the Millers,* chapter 15

❑ *Stories From Around the World:* "Snake Charmer" (Usborne)

❑ *To the Top* – S.A. Kramer

❑ *Little Black Sambo* – Helen Bannerman

❑ *The Story of Little Babaji* – Helen Bannerman

❑ *Adventures of Mohan* – Rod and Staff

❑ *One Grain of Rice* – Demi

❑ *Magical Tales from Many Lands* – Margeret Mayo, "The Prince and the Flying Carpet"

❑ *Nursery Tales Around the World* – Judy Sierra, "The Cat and the Parrot"

❑ Indian Folk Tales
  • http://hazel.forest.net/whootie/stories/india_pansa_h.html
  • http://hazel.forest.net/whootie/stories/six_judges_india.html
  • http://hazel.forest.net/whootie/stories/wali_dad_india.html

Language Arts

❑ Choose from the Language Arts Suggestions on page 6.

❑ India is one of many countries that have a special day to honor and celebrate children. Let your child write (or dictate) a paragraph describing a special day for children in America and include the date, what types of food, games, and ceremonies they would want to occur on this special day.

Science

❑ Elephant
  • *Considering God's Creation,* lesson 20
  • *Pocket Factfiles: Mammals,* pages 126–127
  • *Zoo Guide,* page 37
  • *Elephants* – Louise Martin
  • *Little Big Ears* – Cynthia Moss (This is a wonderful story of a baby elephant's first year of life. Since it is set in Africa, you may use it here or in the study of Africa.)
  • www.enchantedlearning.com/subjects/mammals/elephant/
  • http://coloring-page.net/activity/pages/dot-2.html
  • http://elephant.elehost.com/

❑ Tiger
  • *Pocket Factfiles: Mammals,* pages 12–13
  • *Magnificent Mammals,* page 62
  • *Zoo Guide,* page 173
  • *Tigers* – Louise Martin
  • www.enchantedlearning.com/subjects/mammals/tiger/index.shtml
  • www.indiantiger.org/wild-cats/tiger.html
  • http://kids.nationalgeographic.com/Animals/CreatureFeature/Tiger
  • http://animals.nationalgeographic.com/animals/mammals/bengal-tiger.html

❑ Water Buffalo
  - *Pocket Factfiles: Mammals,* pages 154–155
  - www.animalinfo.org/species/artiperi/bubaarne.htm
  - http://animals.nationalgeographic.com/animals/mammals/water-buffalo.html
❑ Chevrotain
  - www.encyclopedia.com/topic/chevrotain.aspx

Activities

❑ Color or make the flag of India.

❑ Color or label a map of India.

❑ Label the Arabian Sea and the Bay of Bengal on a world map.

❑ Make Indian Flat Bread.

2 cups all-purpose flour	¼ cup plain yogurt
1 egg, slightly beaten	1½ teaspoons baking powder
1 teaspoon sugar	¼ teaspoon salt
⅛ teaspoon baking soda	½ cup milk
oil	poppy seeds

Directions: Mix all ingredients except milk, oil, and poppy seeds. Stir in enough milk to make a soft dough. Turn dough onto lightly floured surface. Knead until smooth, about 5 minutes. Place in greased bowl; turn greased side up. Cover, let rest in warm place 3 hours until doubled. Divide dough into 6 or 8 equal parts. Flatten each part on lightly floured surface, rolling it out to 6″×4″, ¼ inch thick. Brush with oil; sprinkle with poppy seeds. Place 2 cookie sheets in oven; heat oven to 450°F. Remove cookie sheets from oven; place breads on hot cookie sheets. Bake 6–8 minutes.

❑ Make an Indian meal from *Eat Your Way Around the World*.

❑ Play Parcheesi (which has its origins in India).

❑ Go to www.crayola.com/activitybook/print.cfm?id=1032 for a Rangoli craft.

Bible

❑ *Missionary Stories with the Millers,* chapter 15
  - Luke 8:22–25

❑ *Missionary Stories with the Millers,* chapter 20
  - Isaiah 61:1
  - Luke 4:18

❑ *Missionary Stories with the Millers,* chapter 23
  - Isaiah 54:6a
  - Matthew 28:19

Holidays and Celebrations

- *Food and Festivals: India* – Mike Hirst
- www.indianholiday.com/theme-holidays-in-india/
- www.sscnet.ucla.edu/southasia/Culture/Festivals/Dusseh.html
- http://festivals.iloveindia.com/
- www.thebestofindia.com/holiday.asp

Travel and Tourism

Government of India Tourist Office
1270 Avenue of the Americas, Suite 1808
New York, NY 10020

Telephone: 212-586-4901
Telephone: 1-800-953-9399 (toll-free in USA)

Email: ny@itonyc.com
Website: www.tourismofindia.com/

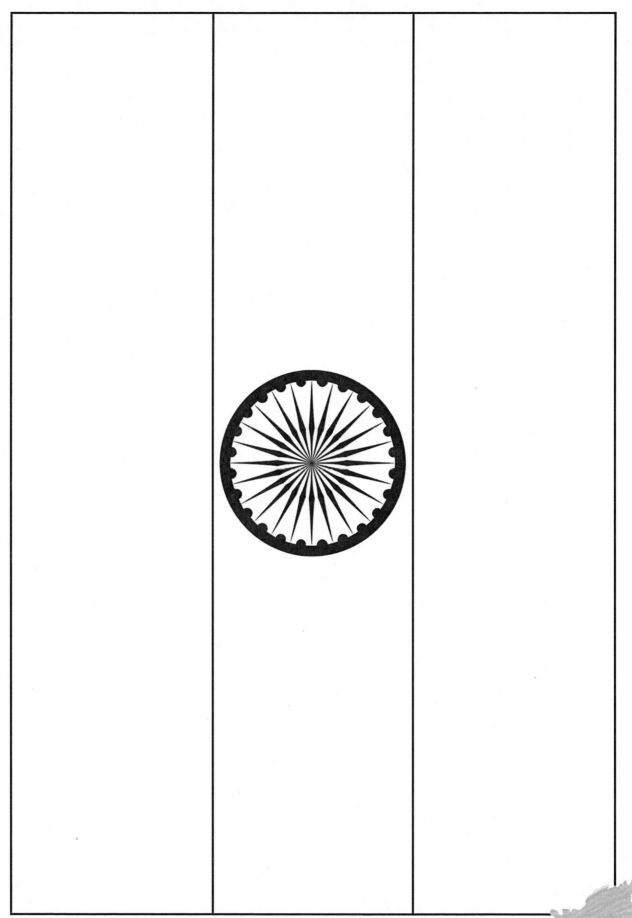

Flag of India

India

connect the dots

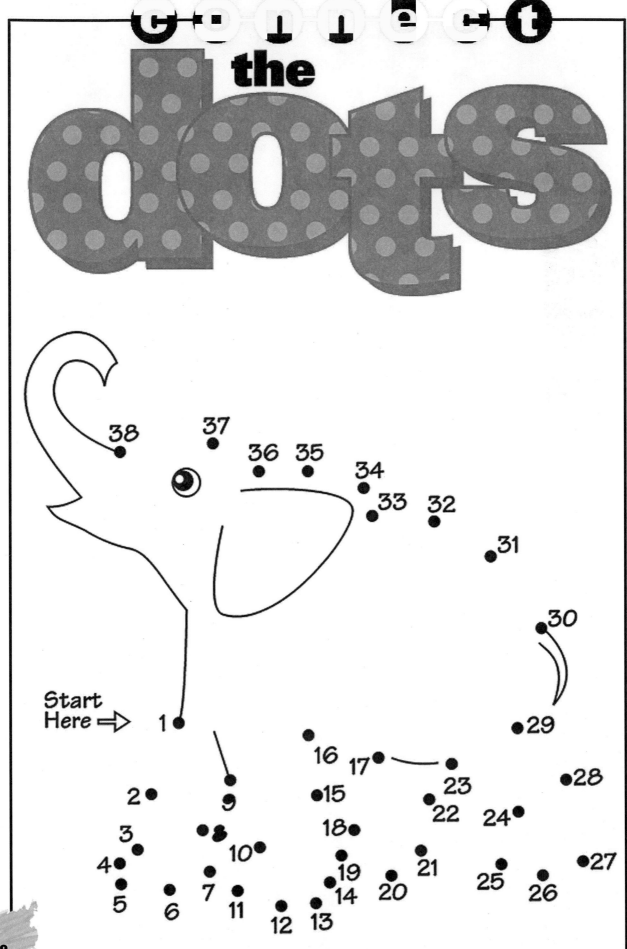

Start Here ⇒

India

FIND THE TWINS.

WHICH TWO ARE EXACTLY ALIKE?

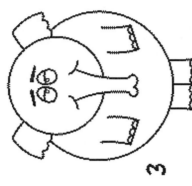

3

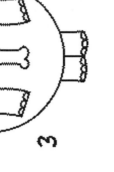

2

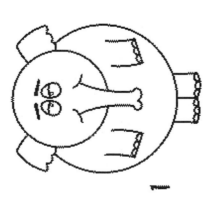

1

4

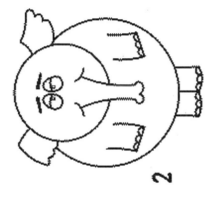

6

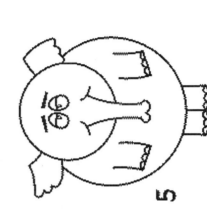

5

49

India

Israel

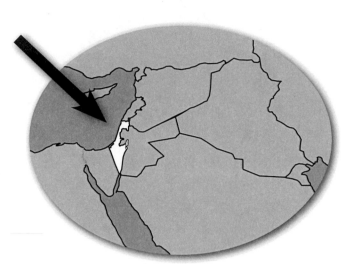

The Middle East

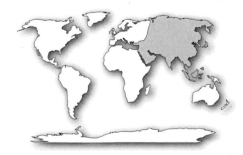

Population _____

Capital City _____

Religion _____

Type of Government _____

Currency _____

Language _____

What are the people called? _____

50

Israel

Israel

Although it was not officially recognized as a nation until 1948, Israel is the land that God promised to His chosen people, the Jews. Its capital, Jerusalem, is considered the holiest city in the world. Many world religions have teachings that center on events that took place in Jerusalem.

The flag of Israel is a Star of David and two blue stripes on a field of white. The Star of David is an ancient emblem of the Jewish people. The blue and white are taken from the *tallit*, the Jewish prayer shawl.

Jews and Arabs both claim Israel as their homeland because both groups trace their ancestry back to Abraham. The Jews are the descendants of Isaac, the son of Abraham and his wife, Sarah. The Arabs are the descendants of Ishmael, the son of Abraham and Sarah's servant, Hagar. These two groups have been fighting over the land that Israel occupies for thousands of years.

In 1949 Israel signed the Armistice Agreement with its neighbors, Jordan, Egypt, Syria, and Lebanon, ending the Arab-Israeli War. The boundaries established by this agreement were ceasefire lines; they did not become Israel's permanent borders until 1979.

History and Biographies

- ❑ Jesus
- ❑ Abraham
- ❑ Isaac
- ❑ Jacob
- ❑ Children of Israel as God's chosen people
- ❑ David Ben-Gurion – the "Father of Modern Israel"
- ❑ Golda Meir – Israel's first female Prime Minister

General References

- ❑ *Passport to Israel* – Clive Lawton
- ❑ *We Live in Israel* – Gemma Levine
- ❑ *Take a Trip to Israel* – Jonathan Rutland
- ❑ *A Kibbutz in Israel* – Allegra Taylor
- ❑ *Count Your Way Through Israel* – James Haskins
- ❑ *A Kid's Catalog of Israel* – Chaya M. Burstein
- ❑ *Hanukkah* – Lola M. Schaefer
- ❑ *Dance, Sing, Remember* – Leslie Kimmelman
- ❑ *Children Just Like Me*, pages 60–61

Literature

- *Mrs. Katz and Tush* – Patricia Polacco
- *Matzah Ball* – Mindy Avra Portnoy
- *Sammy Spider's First Shabbat* – Sylvia A. Rouss
- *Sammy Spider's First Passover* – Sylvia A. Rouss
- *Sammy Spider's First Hanukkah* – Sylvia A. Rouss
- *Joseph Who Loved the Sabbath* – Marilyn Hirsh
- *Magical Tales from Many Lands* – Margeret Mayo, "Seven Clever Brothers"

Language Arts

- Choose from the Language Arts Suggestions on page 6.
- Make a Venn diagram comparing characteristics of donkeys and horses. (A Venn Diagram is a graphic organizer. To download a free copy go to: http://www.edhelper.com/teachers/Sorting_graphic_organizers.htm.)

Science

- Donkey
  - www.enchantedlearning.com/subjects/mammals/horse/Donkeyprintout.shtml

Activities

- Color or make the flag of Israel.
- Color or label a map of Israel.
- Label the Mediterranean Sea on a world map.
- Listen to Jewish music. Check your local library for selections or go to http://en.wikipedia.org/wiki/Music_of_Israel.
- Make a Jewish meal from *Eat Your Way Around the World*.
- Read *Jewish Holiday Games for Little Hands* by Ruth Esrig Brinn.
- Make an Israeli meal.
- Go to www.enchantedlearning.com/themes/hebrew.shtml for printable activity pages.

Bible

- The story of Abraham
  - Genesis 12–13
  - Genesis 15
  - Genesis 17–18
  - Genesis 21–22
- The story of Isaac
  - Genesis 21:1–5
  - Genesis 24
  - Genesis 25:19–28:5

- ❑ The story of Jacob
  - Genesis 25:19–34
  - Genesis 27–35
  - Genesis 46–50
- ❑ *Mrs. Katz and Tush*
  - Leviticus 19:18
  - Psalm 87
  - Matthew 7:12
  - Matthew 22:39
  - Luke 6:31
  - Luke 10:27
- ❑ Donkey
  - Genesis 22:3
  - Job 6:5
  - Job 39:5–8
  - Proverbs 26:3
  - Matthew 21:1–7

Holidays and Celebrations

- ❑ http://en.wikipedia.org/wiki/Public_holidays_in_Israel
- ❑ www.worldwide-tax.com/israel/isrholidays.asp
- ❑ www.jewfaq.org/holidayf.htm

Travel and Tourism

Israel Government Tourist Office
6380 Wilshire Blvd, Suite 1700
Los Angeles, CA 90048

Telephone: 323-658-7463
Telephone: 1-888-77-ISRAEL (toll-free in USA)

Email: igtowest@yahoo.com

Website: www.goisrael.com

Flag of Israel

Israel

Word Search

```
i  s  r  a  e  l  d  a  u
j  u  p  x  n  y  n  s  q
k  o  r  e  a  j  p  i  e
k  n  m  a  e  e  c  a  q
e  k  y  g  a  v  h  n  c
x  z  j  a  p  a  n  v  h
o  o  t  b  h  n  m  r  i
n  q  v  j  c  a  u  t  n
i  n  d  i  a  o  q  h  a
```

Asia   China
India   Israel
Japan   Korea

Asia Review Map

See how many countries you can identify. Write their names on the map.

© 2003 Geography Matters

ad majorem Dei gloriam!

Europe

Europe is the smallest inhabited continent, but it has the third largest population. Europe is a very diverse continent with many different cultures. The terrain varies from vast, rich farmland to splendid, towering mountains. The highest point in Europe is in Russia at Mt El'brus (18,510 ft) and the lowerst point is in the Caspian Sea (92 ft. below sea level). Russia is located on both Europe and Asia maps. For this study, it is covered in Europe.

Europe

Color each country you study.

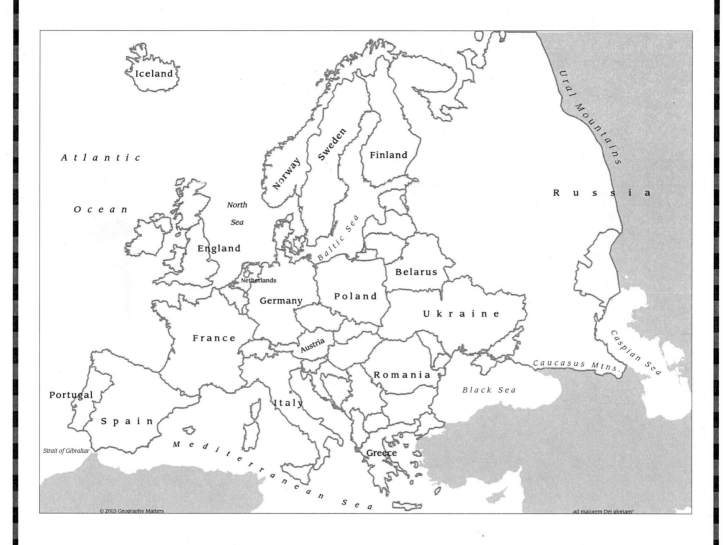

Iceland

Atlantic

Ocean

North
Sea

England

Netherlands

Germany

France

Portugal

Spain

Strait of Gibraltar

M e d i t e r r a n e a n   S e a

Norway

Sweden

Finland

Baltic Sea

Poland

Belarus

Austria

Italy

Romania

Greece

Ukraine

Ural Mountains

R u s s i a

Caspian Sea

Caucasus Mtns.

Black Sea

© 2003 Geography Matters

ad maiorem Dei gloriam!

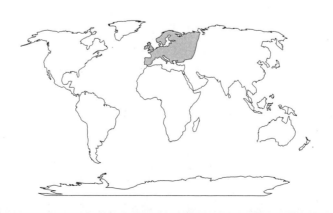

Russia

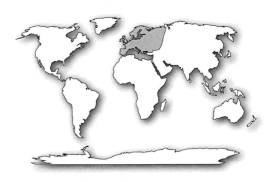

Population _____

Capital City _____

Religion _____

Type of Government _____

Currency _____

Language _____

What are the people called? _____

60

Russia

Russia

The largest country in the world, Russia is actually on two continents, Europe and Asia. The Ural Mountains in western Russia are considered the dividing line between the two continents. Moscow is the capital of Russia.

Russian czars once had complete control of the country. Many of them were harsh rulers that kept Russia cut off from the rest of the world. As a result, Russia was a poor country that fell behind other countries in industry and technology. This set the stage for a revolution in 1917 that removed the czar from power. Unfortunately, the revolution merely took the Russian people from one dictatorship to another. Russia became part of the first Communist country known as the Union of Soviet Socialist Republics (USSR). The USSR collapsed in 1991, and Russia once again became an independent country.

The Russian flag is a tricolor of white, blue, and red. The flag was originally adopted in 1799, but was replaced by the hammer and cycle flag of the USSR in 1922. The tricolor flag was restored when the USSR collapsed in 1991.

Geography

- ❑ Ural Mountains
- ❑ Tundra
  - *Geography from A to Z,* page 43

History and Biographies

- ❑ Catherine the Great
- ❑ Peter Tchaikovsky
  - *Tchaikovsky Discovers America* – Classical Kids audio series
  - *The Story of Tchaikovsky* – Music Masters Series (audio)
  - *Getting to Know the World's Greatest Composers: Tchaikovsky* – Mike Venezia
  - *The Nutcracker* – Carin Dewhirst
- ❑ Peter the Great
  - *Peter the Great* – Diane Stanley
- ❑ Yuri Gagarin
  - www.enchantedlearning.com/explorers/page/g/gagarincloze.shtml

General References

- ❑ *Next Stop Russia* – Clare Boast
- ❑ *Cities of the World: St. Petersburg* – Deborah Kent
- ❑ *Eyewitness Books: Russia* – Kathleen Berton Murrell

- *Russia* – Kristin Thoennes
- *Look What Came From Russia* – Miles Harvey
- *Russia* – Bob Italia
- *Russia* – Susan H. Gray
- *Russian Federation* (A True Book) – Karen Jacobsen
- *Children Just Like Me,* pages 30–31

Literature

- *Another Celebrated Dancing Bear* – Gladys Scheffrin-Falk
- *The Peddler's Gift* – Maxine Rose Schur
- *The Fool of the World and the Flying Ship:* A Russian Folktale
- *The Cat and the Cook* – Ethel Heins
- *Good Morning Chick* – M. Ginsburg
- *My Mother is the Most Beautiful Woman in the World* – Becky Reyher
- *The Mitten* – Jan Brett
- *The Gossipy Wife* – Amanda Hall
- *One Fine Day* – Hogrogrian
- *Clever Katya* – Mary Hoffman
- *Favorite Fairy Tales Told in Russia* – Virginia Haviland

Language Arts

- Choose from the Language Arts Suggestions on page 6.

Science

- *Considering God's Creation,* lesson 22
- Bears
  - *Pocket Factfiles: Mammals,* pages 40–41
  - *Zoo Guide,* pages 25-27
  - *Baby Grizzly* – Beth Spanijian
  - *Grizzly Bear* – Berniece Freschet
  - *Bear* – Mike Down
  - *Bears* (A New True Book) – Mark Rosenthal
  - http://kids.nationalgeographic.com/Animals/CreatureFeature/Brown-bear
- Wolf
  - *Zoo Guide,* page 49
  - *Watchful Wolves* – Ruth Berman
  - *Wolves* – Karen Dudley
  - *Look to the North: A Wolf Pup Diary* – Jean Craighead George
  - *Pocket Factfiles: Mammals,* pages 26–27
  - *Reading About the Gray Wolf* – Carol Greene
  - http://kids.nationalgeographic.com/Animals/CreatureFeature/Graywolf

Activities

❑ Make pretzels.

1 envelope dry yeast	1½ cups lukewarm water
¾ teaspoon salt	1½ teaspoons sugar
4 cups flour	1 egg, beaten
coarse (kosher) salt	

Directions: In a large bowl, dissolve yeast in water. Add sugar and salt. Mix in flour and knead until the dough is soft and smooth. Do not let dough rise. Divide immediately into smaller pieces and roll into ropes. Form the ropes into circles or pretzel shapes. Place on a cookie sheet covered with foil and dusted with flour. Brush each pretzel with the beaten egg mixed with a little water and sprinkle with coarse salt. Bake in a 400°F oven until brown.

(Pretzels are a common food in Russia. They have pretzel carts the way our major cities have hot dog carts.)

❑ Go to the ballet or rent a video of *The Nutcracker*.

❑ Listen to Tchaikovsky.

❑ Color or make the flag of Russia.

❑ Color or label a map of Russia.

❑ Label the Ural Mountains and the Sea of Okhotsk on a world map.

❑ Make a Russian meal from *Eat Your Way Around the World*.

❑ Go to www.crayola.com/activitybook/print.cfm?id=1355 for a picture of St. Basil's Cathedral to color.

❑ Go to www.enchantedlearning.com/themes/russia.shtml for printable activities.

Bible

❑ *Another Celebrated Dancing Bear*
   • Proverbs 17:17
   • John 15:12–13

❑ Bears
   • 1 Samuel 17:34–37
   • 2 Samuel 17:8
   • 2 Kings 2:23–25
   • Isaiah 11:7
   • Isaiah 59:11

❑ *One Fine Day*
   • Genesis 47:16–19

❑ Wolf
   • Genesis 49:27
   • Isaiah 11:6
   • Zephaniah 3:1–5
   • Matthew 7:15–20
   • John 10:7–15

❑ *The Mitten*
   • Isaiah 1:18

Holidays and Celebrations

❑ http://en.wikipedia.org/wiki/Public_holidays_in_Russia

❑ www.cp-pc.ca/english/russia/holidays.html

❑ www.russia-ic.com/eng/Travel/holidays.html

Travel and Tourism

Russian National Tourist Office
130 West 42nd Street, Suite 412
New York, NY 10036

Telephone: 1-877-221-7120 (toll-free in USA)
Telephone: 212-575-3431
Email: info@russia-travel.com
Website: www.russia-travel.com

Flag of Russia

64

Russia

Russia

Great Britain

Population _____

Capital City _____

Religion _____

Type of Government _____

Currency _____

Language _____

What are the people called? _____

Great Britain

Great Britain

A small island nation in the north Atlantic, Great Britain once ruled the largest empire in world history. Made up of England, Scotland, Wales, and Northern Ireland, the official name is The United Kingdom of Great Britain and Northern Ireland. It is normally shortened to Great Britain, Britain, United Kingdom, or the UK. The capital city is London.

The flag of Great Britain blends the flags of England and Scotland with the saltire of Ireland's St. Patrick. King James wanted a flag to show the unification of England and Scotland. The flag was designed in 1606 and became known as the Union Jack. St. Andrew's Cross from the flag of Scotland was used as the base because James was the King of Scotland before he was the King of England. The Cross of St. Patrick was added in 1801 with the addition of Ireland to the commonwealth.

Great Britain is famous for its royal family. As a constitutional monarchy, the king or queen is the head of state. While he or she may reign, they do not rule; meaning they have no power to make or change laws. The ability to make or change laws lies with Parliament. Officials known as ministers oversee the government of Great Britain.

Geography
❑ Channel

History and Biographies
❑ William Shakespeare
- *Profiles from History,* page 43
- *Bard of Avon* – Diane Stanley
- *What's Their Story? William Shakespeare* – Haydn Middleton
- www.crayola.com/activitybook/print.cfm?id=642

❑ Elizabeth I
- *Young Queen Elizabeth* – Francine Sabin
- *Good Queen Bess* – Diane Stanley

❑ Charles Dickens
- *The Man Who Had Great Expectations* – Diane Stanley

❑ Beatrix Potter
- *Beatrix Potter* – John Malam
- *Country Artist* – David R. Collins

❑ Florence Nightingale
- *Florence Nightingale* – Young Christian Library
- *Florence Nightingale* – Animated Hero Classics Video

- "The Angel of the Crimea" – *Your Story Hour* (Album 7 Patterns of Destiny)
- *A Picture Book of Florence Nightingale* – David Adler
- *Ten Girls Who Made History* – Irene Howat, pages 35–47

General References

- ❑ *A Family in England* – Jetty St. John
- ❑ *England* (A True Book) – Michael Burgan
- ❑ *Take a Trip to England* – Chris Fairclough
- ❑ *Passport to Great Britain* – Nicola Wright
- ❑ *We Live in Britain* – Chris Fairclough
- ❑ *A Taste of Britain* – Roz Denny
- ❑ *Cooking the English Way* – Barbara W. Hill
- ❑ www.royal.gov.uk
- ❑ www.number-10.gov.uk
- ❑ www.castles-of-britain.com
- ❑ www.britannia.com/history/h6.html

Literature

- ❑ *Tales From Shakespeare* – Charles and Mary Lamb
- ❑ *Shakespeare for Children,* audio by Jim Weiss
- ❑ *Young Persons Guide to Shakespeare* – Anita Ganeri
- ❑ *Tale of Peter Rabbit* – Beatrix Potter
- ❑ *Mr. Gumpy's Motor Car* – John Burningham
- ❑ *Mr. Gumpy's Outing* – John Burningham
- ❑ "My Heart's in the Highlands" – Robert Burns (poem)
- ❑ *Winnie the Pooh* – A. A. Milne
- ❑ *Robin Hood* retold – Margaret Early
- ❑ *St. George and the Dragon* – Margaret Hodges
- ❑ *Stories From Around The World*: "Dick Whittington" (Usborne)
- ❑ *Mary Jones and Her Bible* – Mary Ropes

Language Arts

- ❑ Choose from the Language Arts Suggestions on page 6.
- ❑ Use portions of Shakespeare's poems/plays as copy work.

Science

- ❑ Sheep
  - *Baby Lamb* – Beth Spanjian
  - *Smudge, the Little Lost Lamb* – James Herriot
  - *The Sheep Book* – Dorothy Hinshaw Patent
  - *Sheep* (A True Book) – Sara Swan Miller
  - *Farm Animals* (A New True Book) – Karen Jacobsen, pages 25–30

Great Britain

Activities

- ❑ Color or make the flag of Great Britain.
- ❑ Color or label a map of Great Britain.
- ❑ Label the English Channel on a world map.
- ❑ Listen to a recording of bagpipes (check your local library) or go to http://www.youtube.com/watch?v=f5O0cDpEay8&feature=related.
- ❑ Go to tea at a local teahouse or have a tea party at home.
- ❑ Make an English or Irish meal from *Eat Your Way Around the World*.
- ❑ Although English is spoken in both the United States and Great Britain, not all words are the same. Learn some of these and use them in conversation this week.

bloke – guy	trainers – sneakers	tights – panty hose
mate – friend	ice lolly – popsicle	lift – elevator
petrol – gasoline	telly – television	fringe – bangs
biscuit – cookie	jumper – sweater	bangers – sausages
boot – car trunk	bonnet – hood	I'll ring you – I'll call you
bobby – police officer		

Bible

- ❑ *The Tale of Peter Rabbit*
  - Matthew 26:36
  - Luke 23:43
  - John 19:41
  - John 18:1
  - Ephesians 6:1
  - 2 Timothy 2:6
  - James 5:7

- ❑ Sheep
  - Genesis 4:2–5
  - Exodus 2:16–19
  - 2 Kings 3:4
  - Ezekiel 34
  - Daniel 8:3–8
  - Matthew 10:16
  - Matthew 25:31–33
  - Luke 2:8–20
  - John 1:29

Holidays and Celebrations

- ❑ http://en.wikipedia.org/wiki/UK_national_holidays
- ❑ http://en.wikipedia.org/wiki/List_of_public_holidays_in_Wales
- ❑ www.geocities.com/traditions_uk/

Travel and Tourism

British Tourist Authority
551 Fifth Avenue, Suite 701
New York, NY 10176-0799

Telephone: 1-800-462-2748 (toll-free in USA)
Telephone: 212-986-2266

Email: travelinfo@bta.org.uk
Website: www.visitbritain.com

Flag of Great Britain

Great Britain

Crossword Puzzle

Across
2 Famous forest.
3 River in 1 down.
4 Famous clock in 1 down.
5 Word used for gasoline.
6 Word used for friend.
8 The name of the Queen.

Down
1 The capital of England.
2 Famous playwrite.
7 Animal raised for its wool.

Great Britain

France

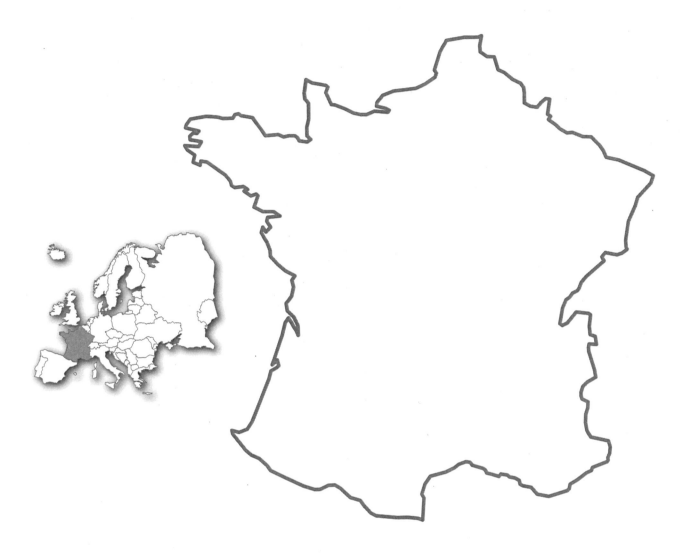

72

Population _____

Capital City _____

Religion _____

Type of Government _____

Currency _____

Language _____

What are the people called? _____

France

France

Twice the size of Colorado, France is a land of beautiful and varied landscapes. Because it has six sides, the French often call their country the hexagon. Paris, the capital of France, is one of the most famous cities in the world.

The French flag is a blue, white, and red tricolor adopted in 1792. Blue stands for the capital city, Paris. White is the color of the deposed royal family, the House of Bourbon. Red represents revolution.

French art and literature have greatly impacted Western culture. The art movement know as Impressionism began in France in the late 19th century and took its name from a painting by Claude Monet. While not as well known for its musical contributions, there are a number of fine French composers, such as Louis Hector Berlioz. To the French, cooking is an art form and French cuisine is world famous.

Geography
❑ Palisade
   • *Geography from A to Z,* page 34

History and Biographies
❑ Marie Curie
   • *Marie Curie: Brave Scientist* – Keith Brandt
   • *Marie Curie's Search For Radium* – Beverley Birch and Christian Birmingham

❑ Louis Pasteur
   • *Louis Pasteur Young Scientist* – Francene Sabin
   • *Pasteur's Fight Against Microbes* – Beverley Birch and Christian Birmingham
   • "Solving the Riddle" – *Your Story Hour* (Album 7 Patterns of Destiny)

❑ Claude Monet
   • *Getting to Know the World's Greatest Artists: Monet* – Mike Venezia
   • *Monet – Jude Welton* (Eyewitness Books by Dorling Kindersly)
   • *Art for Young People: Claude Monet* – Peter Harrison
   • *Monet* – Vanessa Potts (A wonderful book with a photograph of Monet's work on one page and a short discussion or background on the work on the opposite page.)

❑ Joan of Arc
   • *Joan of Arc* – Diane Stanley
   • *Joan of Arc* – Margaret Hodges
   • "The Girl General" – *Your Story Hour* (Album 7 Patterns of Destiny)

General References

- ❑ *Usborne First Book of France*
- ❑ *Cooking the French Way* – Lynne Marie Waldee
- ❑ *France* – Michael Dahl
- ❑ *Picture a Country: France* (Watts Publishing Group)
- ❑ *Look What Came From France* – Miles Harvey
- ❑ *Count Your Way Through France* – Jim Haskins
- ❑ *A Family in France* (Families the World Over series)
- ❑ *Children Just Like Me,* page 32
- ❑ *Looking at France* – Jillian Powell
- ❑ *France* – Cynthia Klingel & Robert B. Noyed
- ❑ *Letters from Around the World: France* – Teresa Fisher

Literature

- ❑ *Giraffe That Walked to Paris* – Nancy Milton
- ❑ *Bon Appetit, Bertie!* – Joan Knight
- ❑ *Mirette on the High Wire* – Emily Arnold McCully
- ❑ *Marie in Fourth Position* – Amy Littlesugar
- ❑ *Madeline* – Ludwig Bemelmans
- ❑ *Puss in Boots* retold – Lorinda Bryan Cauley
- ❑ *Little Red Riding Hood* retold – James Marshall
- ❑ *Three Musketeers* - Jim Weiss audio
- ❑ *New Coat for Anna* – Harriet Ziefert
- ❑ *Linnea in Monet's Garden* – Christina Bjork
- ❑ *Glorious Flight* – Alice and Martin Provensen
- ❑ *Three Sacks of Truth* – Eric A. Kimmel
- ❑ *Paddington Abroad* – Michael Bond
- ❑ *Magical Tales from Many Lands* – Margeret Mayo, "Three Golden Apples"

Language Arts

- ❑ Choose from the Language Arts Suggestions on page 6.
- ❑ Write a paragraph about the Eiffel Tower, or make a list of places in France.
- ❑ Have child make a poster of artists that have works in the Louvre in Paris. Use the matchbook pattern in *Big Book of Books and Activities,* page 31, and then mount them on the poster board. For added practice have the child list the artists in alphabetical order.

Science

- ❑ Trees
  - *1st Nature Trees* (Usborne)
  - *Ultimate Trees and Flowers Sticker Book*
  - *Trees* – Linda Gamlin

- *Oak Trees* – Marcia S. Freeman
- *How a Seed Grows* – Helene J. Jordan
- *Leaves* – Gail Saunders-Smith
- *Why Do Leaves Change Color* – Betsy Maestro
- *The Secret Life of Trees* – Chiara Chevallier
- *Discovering Trees* – Keith Brandt
- *Considering God's Creation*, lesson 11
- *Usborne Internet-linked Science Encyclopedia*, pages 256–265

Activities

❑ Color or make the flag of France.

Cut red, white, and blue paper evenly into thirds. Let the child glue the strips onto a piece of paper or cardboard. Or, divide a piece of paper into thirds with a pencil. Let the child paint the red and blue stripes.

❑ Color or label a map of France.

❑ Label the Bay of Biscay on a world map.

❑ Plant a tree.

❑ Make Chocolate Truffles.

½ cup heavy cream	8 oz chopped, semi-sweet chocolate + 6 oz for dipping
2 T butter	½ cup cocoa powder, sifted
1 teaspoon light corn syrup	

Directions: Combine cream, butter, and corn syrup together in a saucepan. Place over medium heat and bring to a full boil. Turn off heat.

Add 8 ounces of chopped chocolate, and gently swirl the pan. Do not stir. Allow to rest 5 minutes.

After 5 minutes, whisk slowly to combine.

Transfer the mixture to a bowl and refrigerate for 45 minutes, stirring every 15 minutes.

After 45 minutes, the mixture will start to thicken quickly, keep refrigerated another 11 to 15 minutes, stirring every 5 minutes.

Using a mini ice cream scoop or two spoons, form the mixture into 1" balls and place on baking sheets that have been lined with waxed paper. Chill until firm, about 10–15 minutes.

While the balls are chilling, melt the remaining 6 ounces of chocolate. After it is completely melted, allow to cool slightly before continuing.

Place cocoa in small bowl. Remove the balls from the refrigerator. Using one hand, dip the balls into the melted chocolate. Allow the excess to drip back into the bowl. Place the truffle in the cocoa. With your clean hand, cover the truffle with cocoa.

Lift it out and place on the baking sheet. Repeat with the remaining truffles. Place back in the refrigerator for 5–8 minutes to set.

May be stored up to one week in an airtight container.

❑ Make a French meal from *Eat Your Way Around the World*.

❑ Go to http//www.crayola.com/activitybook/print.cfm?id=576 for a coloring page of the Eiffel Tower.

❑ Go to www.enchantedlearning.com/europe/france/index.shtml for printable activities.

Bible

- ❑ *The Giraffe That Walked to Paris*
  - Proverbs 12:10
  - Proverbs 16:21
  - Proverbs 25:11
  - Psalm 40:1
  - Matthew 5:23–24
  - 2 Corinthians 5:18
  - Colossians 1:11
  - James 1:4

- ❑ *Bon Appetit, Bertie!*
  - I Corinthians 10:31

- ❑ *Mirette on the High Wire*
  - Jeremiah 29:11

- ❑ *Marie in Fourth Position*
  - Ecclesiastes 7:8
  - Romans 2:7
  - Romans 5:3
  - Colossians 1:9–11
  - James 1:3
  - I Thessalonians 5:14

- ❑ *Madeline*
  - Proverbs 1:10
  - Acts 9:36
  - I Corinthians 14:40
  - Colossians 3:12
  - Philippians 4:8
  - I Peter 3:10–12

- ❑ *Linnea in Monet's Garden*
  - Proverbs 12:27
  - Matthew 25:1–30
  - Colossians 3:23

- ❑ *The Glorious Flight*
  - 2 Chronicles 15:7
  - Psalm 127
  - Psalm 128

- ❑ *A New Coat for Anna*
  - Exodus 36:7–8
  - Proverbs 23:5
  - Matthew 6:8
  - Matthew 6:19
  - Mark 12:31–44
  - Philippians 4:19

- ❑ *Trees*
  - Genesis 2:8–9
  - Genesis 8:10–12
  - Judges 9:8–15
  - 2 Samuel 6:5
  - I Kings 6:23, 31, 33
  - I Kings 10:11–12
  - I Chronicles 14:14–15
  - 2 Chronicles 2:8–9
  - Nehemiah 8:15–16
  - Psalm 1
  - Psalm 104:16–17
  - Isaiah 2:12–18
  - Isaiah 41:19
  - Isaiah 44:13–20
  - Isaiah 60:13
  - Ezekiel 17:22–24
  - Ezekiel 27:4–6
  - Ezekiel 31:1–9
  - Joel 1:12
  - Zechariah 1:8–11
  - Luke 13:6–9
  - Luke 19:1–10
  - John 12:12–13
  - James 3:10–12

Holidays and Celebrations

- ❑ http://en.wikipedia.org/wiki/Holidays_in_France
- ❑ www.discoverfrance.net/France/DF_holidays.shtml

Travel and Tourism

French Government Tourist Office
444 Madison Avenue, 16th Floor
New York, NY 10022-6903

Telephone: 212-838-7800
Email: info.us@franceguide.com
Website: www.franceguide.com

Flag of France

France

77

Crossword Puzzle

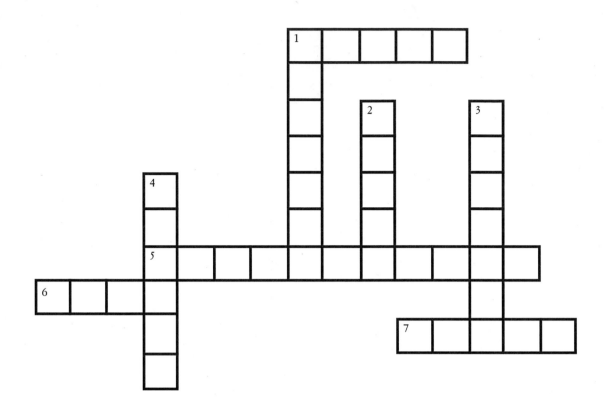

Across

1 Capital of France.
5 Famous landmark in 1 across.
6 First name of girl burned at the stake.
7 Scientist that worked with radium.

Down

1 France is known for this product.
2 Famous painter.
3 Scientist who studied microbes.
4 Language spoken in France.

France

France

Italy

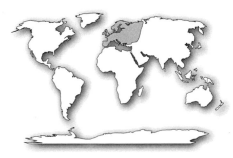

Population _____

Capital City _____

Religion _____

Type of Government _____

Currency _____

Language _____

What are the people called? _____

80

Italy

Italy

About the size of Arizona, Italy looks like a boot kicking a stone. The name, given by the ancient Romans, means "land of oxen" or "grazing land." Rome, the capital of Italy, has been at the center of world affairs for thousands of years. Vatican City, the smallest independent country in the world, lies completely within Rome. The headquarters of the Roman Catholic Church, Vatican City is under the complete authority of the pope.

The flag of Italy is a green, white, and red vertical tricolor. Based on the French flag designed by Napoleon, green replaced the blue because green was reportedly Napoleon's favorite color.

Italy is known throughout the world for its art, architecture, and food. Two of the greatest artists in history, Leonardo da Vinci and Michelangelo, were Italian. The Roman Colosseum, Pantheon, and Leaning Tower of Pisa attract millions of visitors each year. Italy has also given us spaghetti, lasagna, and many other wonderful dishes.

History and Biographies

❑ Michelangelo
  - *Profiles from History*, page 35
  - *Getting to Know the World's Greatest Artists: Michelangelo* – Mike Venezia
  - *Michael the Angel* – Laura Fischetto
  - *Michelangelo's Surprise* – Tony Parillo

❑ Leonardo Da Vinci
  - *Profiles from History*, page 27
  - *Getting to Know the World's Greatest Artists: Da Vinci* – Mike Venezia
  - *Leonardo Da Vinci* – Diane Stanley

❑ Galileo
  - *Profiles from History*, page 61
  - *Starry Messenger* – Peter Sis

❑ Giotto
  - *Getting to Know the World's Greatest Artists: Giotto* – Mike Venezia
  - *A Boy Named Giotto* – Paolo Guarnieri

General References

❑ *Passport to Italy* – Cinzia Mariella

❑ *A Family in Italy* – Penny Hubley

❑ *Italy* – Kristin Thoennes

❑ *Look What Came From Italy* – Miles Harvey

❑ *Next Stop Italy* – Clare Boast

- *Italy* – Mary Berendes
- *Looking at Italy* – Jillian Powell

Literature

- *Papa Piccolo* – Carol Talley
- *Stories From Around the World:* "Buried Treasure" (Usborne)
- *St. Francis and the Friendly Beasts* – Margaret Hodges
- *Antonio's Apprenticeship* – Taylor Morrison
- *Clown of God* – Tomie de Paola
- *Papa Gatto* – Ruth Sanderson
- *The Thread of Life* – Domenico Vittorini
- *Nursery Tales Around the World* – Judy Sierra, "The Rooster and the Mouse"

Language Arts

- Choose from the Language Arts Suggestions on page 6.
- Write or dictate a report on one of the famous people studied from Italy.
- Make a layered book of the Solar System. Refer to the *Big Book of Books and Activities*, page 70.

Science

- Astronomy
  - *Considering God's Creation,* lesson 2
  - *Considering God's Creation,* lesson 3
  - *Looking at the Planets* – Melvin Berger
  - *Find the Constellations* – H.A. Rey
  - *The Sun* – Kate Petty
  - *Journeys to the Edge of Creation* – videos by Moody Institute of Science
  - *Usborne Internet-linked Science Encyclopedia,* pages 154–177
  - www.enchantedlearning.com/themes/astronomy.shtml

Activities

- Color or make the flag of Italy. See France for ideas (use red, white, and green).
- Color or label a map of Italy.
- Label the Adriatic, Ionian, and Tyrrhenian Seas on a world map.
- Learn Roman numerals.
- Paint.

  If studying Michelangelo, tape a large piece of paper under a low table and have the children paint while lying on their back. (Recommend doing this activity outside!)

- Listen to *The Story of Verdi* – Music Masters Series (audio).
- Make an Italian meal from *Eat Your Way Around the World*.
- San Marino, the world's smallest and oldest republic, lies within Italy. For a printable flag to color, go to the www.crayola.com/activitybook/print.cfm?id=1025 website.
- Go to www.enchantedlearning.com/europe/italy/index.shtml for information and printable activities.

Bible

- ❑ *Papa Piccolo*
  - Psalm 68:5
  - James 1:27
- ❑ *Antonio's Apprenticeship*
  - Ecclesiastes 9:10
  - Romans 12:11
  - Colossians 3:22
- ❑ *Clown of God*
  - Psalm 103:2
  - Proverbs 19:17
- ❑ For studying astronomy:
  - Genesis 1:14–19
  - Joshua 10:12–14
  - 2 Samuel 23:4
  - Job 9:9
  - Job 38:31–33
  - Psalm 147:4
  - Psalm 19:6
  - Ecclesiastes 1:5
  - Jeremiah 31:35
  - Amos 5:8
  - Matthew 2:2, 9, 10
  - 1 Corinthians 15:41

Holidays and Celebrations

- ❑ http://en.wikipedia.org/wiki/Holidays_in_Italy
- ❑ www.intlecorner.com/italy/itaholid.php3

Travel and Tourism

Italian Government Tourist Board
630 Fifth Avenue, Suite 1565
New York NY 10111

Telephone: 212-245-4822

Email: enitny@italiantourism.com

Website: www.italiantourism.com

Flag of Italy

Italy

FIND THE TWINS!

WHICH TWO ARE EXACTLY ALIKE?

3

6

2

5

1

4

85

Italy

MAZE CRAZE

Start Here →

Italy

Word Search

```
p l u t o n q a s e k u c k r v z x o k
m a r s v f a o d x f d s z n z d l r v
w o h z a s t e r o i d f v g h a a b t
f m m w k h y m w p a m v y o p j e i n
s i y m e r c u r y e k j o p l j d t l
r l b o h w b s w e r b l f k a y d j u
w k s x m a r x v z m o o n o n j g p s
s y i q e t u r k j j c w u x e q p o o
h w f c t f v u g z c m h e a t j g x l
r a m q e d n e p t u n e k e p s z e a
s y z p o y t g p k j k f p o p s v n r
f c k x r y o i e y t e s c x w a q f s
v i h d i p x e a r t h a o t j t d v y
a n d f t i d r k d x a n m e o u s z s
c e q w e q a s t a r l e e w j r b b t
q z y l t a d b n g k r f t b y n q p e
i u r a n u s v p c l d w h z t m t o m
k x y y y z o i d u f p k a e m d o b u
o x h b n g n c e m j u p i t e r f a v
v e n u s e y t x g z w x i v y p e y q
```

asteroid
comet
Earth
Jupiter
Mars
Mercury
meteorite
Milky Way
moon

Neptune
orbit
planet
Pluto
Saturn
solar system
star
Uranus
Venus

87

Italy

Crossword Puzzle

Across

1 The second planet from the sun.
3 The red planet.
4 The seventh planet from the sun.
7 Our galaxy.
8 The largest planet.
9 This planet has rings.
10 The planet closest to the sun.
12 Any of the thousands of small rocklike or metallic planets that orbit the sun, mostly between Mars and Jupiter.
13 A heavenly body that orbits around a star, such as the sun.
14 A mass of ice, frozen gasses, and dust particles that travels around the sun in a long, slow path.

Down

2 The eighth planet from the sun.
3 A heavenly body that revolves around a planet.
5 The sun together with the planets and other heavenly bodies that it orbits.
6 A heavenly body that shines by its own light.
11 The third planet from the sun.
13 The smallest planet.

Italy

Italy

Germany

Population _____

Capital City _____

Religion _____

Type of Government _____

Currency _____

Language _____

What are the people called? _____

Germany

Germany

Germany, the most densely populated European country, is made up of sixteen states. Because of its location, it has more neighbors than any other European country—nine in all. Germany has made notable contributions to music and science. The capital of Germany is Berlin.

The German flag is a black, red, and gold horizontal tricolor. The colors come from uniforms worn by German soldiers during the Napoleonic Wars.

Prior to 1871, the land that is now Germany was divided into separate kingdoms, dukedoms, and city-states. These principalities were united into a single nation by Otto von Bismarck, the Prime Minister of Prussia. They remained united until the end of World War II when the country was divided into two countries, East Germany and West Germany. They were once again reunited in 1990 with the fall of Communism.

History and Biographies

❑ Ludwig Van Beethoven
- *Ludwig Van Beethoven: Musical Pioneer* – Carol Greene
- *Beethoven: Getting to Know the World's Greatest Composers* – Mike Venezia
- *Beethoven Lives Upstairs* – Classical Kids Audio
- *Ludwig Beethoven and the Chiming Tower Bells* – Opal Wheeler

❑ Johannes Gutenberg
- *Profiles from History*, page 19
- *Gutenberg* – Leonard Everett Fisher

❑ Albert Einstein
- *Young Albert Einstein* – Laurence Santrey
- *Albert Einstein* – Ibi Lepscky
- *Albert Einstein: Young Thinker* – Marie Hammontree
- www.crayola.com/activitybook/print.cfm?id=550

❑ Johann Sebastian Bach
- *Mr. Bach Comes to Call* – Classical Kids Audio
- *Getting to Know the World's Greatest Composers: Bach* – Mike Venezia
- *Sebastian: A Book About Bach* – Jeanette Winter
- *Sebastian Bach, the Boy from Thuringia* – Opal Wheeler and Sybil Deucher
- www.enchantedlearning.com/music/bios/bach/index.shtml

❑ Brahms
- *Getting to Know the World's Greatest Composers: Brahms* – Mike Venezia
- *The Story of Brahms* – Music Masters Series (audio)

- ❑ Handel
  - *Profiles from History*, page 105
  - *Handel and the Famous Sword Swallower of Halle* – Bryna Stevens
  - *The Duke's Command* – Phyllis Berk
  - *Hallelujah Handel* – Classical Kids Audio
  - *Handel at the Court of Kings* – Opal Wheeler
- ❑ Castles
  - *Castles* – Gillian Osband and Robert Andrew
  - *Castles* – Gallimard Jeunesse
  - *Castle Life* – Struan Reid
  - *Incredible Castles and Knights* – Christopher Maynard
  - *How Castles Were Built* – Peter Hicks
- ❑ Robert Schumann
  - *Robert Schumann and Mascot Ziff* – Opal Wheeler

General References

- ❑ *Usborne's First Book of Germany* (Usborne)
- ❑ *Count Your Way Through Germany* – Jim Haskins
- ❑ *Picture A Country: Germany* – Henry Pluckrose
- ❑ *Next Stop Germany* – Clare Boast
- ❑ *Germany* – Mary Berendes
- ❑ *A Family in West Germany* – Ann Adler
- ❑ *Looking at Germany* – Kathleen Pohl
- ❑ *A Look at Germany* – Helen Frost
- ❑ *Germany* – Cath Senker
- ❑ *Germany* – Michael Dahl

Literature

- ❑ *Stories From Around the World:* "Musicians of Bremen" (Usborne)
- ❑ *Goldilocks and the Three Bears* retold by Armand Eisen
- ❑ *The Pied Piper* – Robert Browning
- ❑ *Heidi* – Johannes Spyri
- ❑ *The Duchess Bakes a Cake* – Virginia Kahl
- ❑ *Bach's Big Adventure* – Sallie Ketcham

Language Arts

- ❑ Choose from the Language Arts Suggestions on page 6.
- ❑ Make index cards with facts and/or pictures of the famous artists and musicians from Germany. Make a fold box to store them in and decorate the outside. See *Big Book of Books and Activities*, pages 58–60.

Science

❑ *Considering God's Creation,* lesson 10a

Activities

❑ Color or make the flag of Germany. See France for ideas (use red, black, and yellow).

❑ Color or label a map of Germany.

❑ Label the Baltic Sea on a world map.

❑ Listen to music of the composers you have studied.

❑ If you read *The Duchess Bakes a Cake*, bake a cake.

❑ Make a German meal from *Eat Your Way Around the World*.

❑ Go to www.enchantedlearning.com/themes/german.shtml for printable activities.

❑ Go to www.enchantedlearning.com/music/index.shtml for printable music activities.

❑ Go to www.enchantedlearning.com/themes/castle.shtml for printable castle pages and craft ideas.

❑ Castle maze:
  • http://coloring-page.net/activity/pages/maze-19.html
  • http://coloring-page.net/activity/pages/maze-36.html

Bible

❑ The Bible has a lot to say about music and instruments. Studying the composers is a good time to study what God has to say about music.

  • Exodus 15:20–21
  • 1 Samuel 10:6
  • 2 Samuel 6:5
  • 1 Chronicles 6:32
  • 1 Chronicles 13:8
  • 1 Chronicles 15:11–16:43
  • 1 Chronicles 25:6
  • 2 Chronicles 5:13
  • 2 Chronicles 7:6
  • Nehemiah 12:27
  • Psalm 33:1–3
  • Psalm 96:1
  • Psalm 98:4–6
  • Psalm 147:7
  • Psalm 149:1–5
  • Psalm 150
  • Isaiah 38:20
  • Habakkuk 3:19

❑ *The Duchess Bakes a Cake*
  • Galatians 6:7

Holidays and Celebrations

❑ www.germanculture.com.ua/library/links/holidays.htm

❑ www.germanways.com/Deutsch3.1.htm

Travel and Tourism

German National Tourist Office
122 East 42nd Street
New York, NY 10168-0072

Telephone: 212-661-7200

Email: gntonyc@d-z-t.com

Website: www.cometogermany.com

Flag of Germany

Germany

WHICH TWO ARE EXACTLY ALIKE?

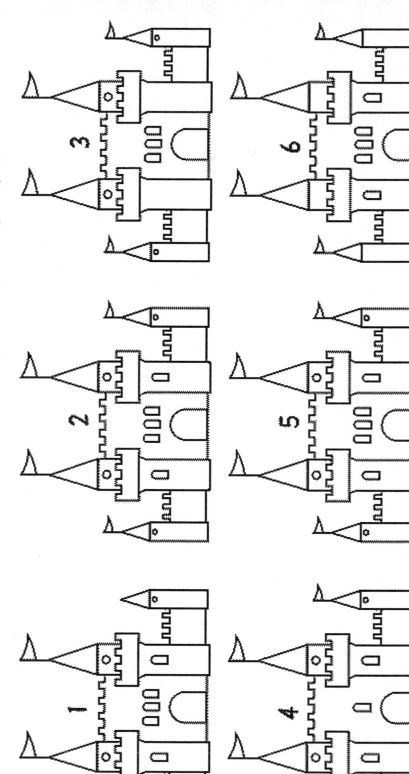

Germany

MAZE CRAZE

Start Here
Find the black note.

Germany

Netherlands

Population _____

Capital City _____

Religion _____

Type of Government _____

Currency _____

Language _____

What are the people called? _____

98

Netherlands

A small, low-lying country the size of Maryland, the Netherlands is frequently referred to as "Holland." (Holland is actually a region in the central-western part of the Netherlands which includes the provinces of North Holland and South Holland). Almost half of the Netherlands lies below sea-level. Low lying areas reclaimed by the sea are called polders. Polders are protected by dikes and are continually being drained by mechanical pumps. The capital city of Amsterdam is built on a polder. The Netherlands along with Belgium and Luxembourg, form the area of Europe known as "The Low Countries."

The flag of the Netherlands is a red, white, and blue horizontal tricolor. Originally the colors were orange, white, and blue to honor William of Orange, the first ruler of the Dutch Republic. During the 16th and 17th centuries the dye that was used for orange eventually turned red, so in the mid-1600s, the orange stripe was officially made a red stripe.

The Netherlands is world famous for its tulips, a member of the lily family. The name tulip means "turban" or "Turk's cap." The Dutch take horticulture very seriously and a new type of tulip is often the result of decades of experiments. Introduced in the 16th century, tulips became such a craze that outrageous prices were being paid for a single bulb. The market grew so wild in the 17th century—people were going bankrupt from stock speculation—that the government stepped in and regulated the industry.

Geography
❑ Polder

History and Biographies
❑ Rembrandt
   • *Rembrandt: Getting to Know the World's Greatest Artists* – Mike Venezia

❑ Vincent Van Gogh
   • *Art for Young People: Vincent Van Gogh* – Peter Harrison
   • *Van Gogh* – Bruce Bernard (Eyewitness Books by Dorling Kindersley) Note: There are a few nude paintings in this book.
   • *Van Gogh* – Josephine Cutts and James Smith – Like the book *Monet* by Vanessa Potts, this book has a photograph of Van Gogh's work on one page and a short discussion or background on the work on the opposite page. Note: Two of the works shown portray a woman's nude backside.

❑ Johannes Vermeer
   • *Johannes Vermeer* – Mike Venezia

General References
❑ *The Netherlands* (A New True Book) – Karen Jacobsen

❑ *Take a Trip to Holland* – Chris Fairclough

❑ *The Netherlands* – Michael Dahl

Literature

- ❑ *Boy Who Held Back the Sea* – Lenny Hort
- ❑ *Stories From Around the World:* "Brave Hendrick" (Usborne)
- ❑ *Hans Brinker or the Silver Skates* – Mary Mapes Dodge
- ❑ *The Hole in the Dike* – Norma B. Green
- ❑ *The Cow Who Fell in the Canal* – Phyllis Krasilovsky
- ❑ *The Little Riders* – Margaretha Shemin

Language Arts

- ❑ Choose from the Language Arts Suggestions on page 6.
- ❑ Write a poem about tulips and then illustrate it.

Science

- ❑ Flowers
  - *Considering God's Creation,* lesson 10b
  - *Flowers* – Gail Saunders-Smith
  - *Flowers* – Gallimard Jeunesse
  - *Flowers* – David Burnie
  - *Usborne Internet-linked Science Encyclopedia,* pages 270–273
  - www.primarygames.com/science/flowers/coloring.htm
  - www.enchantedlearning.com/themes/flowers.shtml

Activities

- ❑ Color or make the flag of Netherlands.
- ❑ Color or label the map of Netherlands.
- ❑ Label the North Sea on a world map.
- ❑ Make Hutspot.

2 lb. beef brisket	1½ cups water
1 teaspoon salt	4 medium potatoes, diced
4 medium carrots, sliced	3 medium onions, chopped
1½ teaspoons salt	¼ teaspoon pepper
snipped parsley	prepared mustard or horseradish

Directions: Heat beef, water, and 1 teaspoon salt to boiling in Dutch oven; reduce heat. Cover and simmer 1½ hours. Add potatoes, carrots, onion, 1½ teaspoons salt, pepper. Cover and simmer until beef and vegetables are tender, about 45 minutes. Drain meat and vegetables, reserving broth. Mash vegetables; mound on heated platter. Cut beef across grain into thin slices; arrange around vegetables. Garnish with parsley. Serve with reserved broth and mustard or horseradish.

- ❑ Taste Dutch cheeses (Edam, Gouda, etc.).
- ❑ Make cheese.

  Making Cheese, Butter, and Yogurt by Phyllis Hobson is the best resource we have found for this project. It tells you how to make the cheese form and press from materials found around the house. *Cheese Making Made Easy* by Ricki Carroll and Robert Carroll and *Making Great Cheese* by Barbara Ciletti are also good.

❑ Scheveningen, Netherlands has a miniature Dutch village. Use small cartons and boxes to make a miniature village. Go to http://jas.familyfun.go.com/crafts/box-buildings-670852/ or http://www.enchantedlearning.com/crafts/Boxtown.shtml for instructions.

❑ Go bowling; it has its origins in the Netherlands.

❑ Make paper windmills.

❑ Make a Dutch meal from *Eat Your Way Around the World*.

❑ Plant tulips.

❑ Go to www.crayola.com/activitybook/print.cfm?id=699 for a coloring page of a windmill.

❑ Go to www.coloring.ws/netherlands.htm for printable coloring pages.

❑ Go to www.enchantedlearning.com/themes/dutch.shtml for printable activities.

Bible

❑ Cheese
- Samuel 17:29
- Job 10:10

❑ Flowers
- Song of Solomon 2:1
- Song of Solomon 6:2
- Isaiah 35:1–2
- Matthew 6:28–29

❑ *Boy Who Held Back the Sea, Brave Hendrick*, and *The Hole in the Dike*
- Psalm 46:1–3
- Psalm 91:5a
- Psalm 118:6a

❑ *The Cow Who Fell in the Canal*
- Psalm 144:15
- Proverbs 3:13
- Proverbs 14:21
- Proverbs 16:20
- Proverbs 28:1

Holidays and Celebrations

❑ *Festivals of the World: Netherlands* – Joyce Van Fenema

❑ http://en.wikipedia.org/wiki/Public_holidays_in_the_Netherlands

Travel and Tourism

Netherlands Board of Tourism
355 Lexington Ave
New York NY 10017

Telephone: 1-888-GO-HOLLAND (toll-free in Canada and USA)
Telephone: 212-557-3500

Email: info@goholland.com

Website: www.holland.com/us/

Flag of Netherlands

Netherlands

MAZE CRAZE

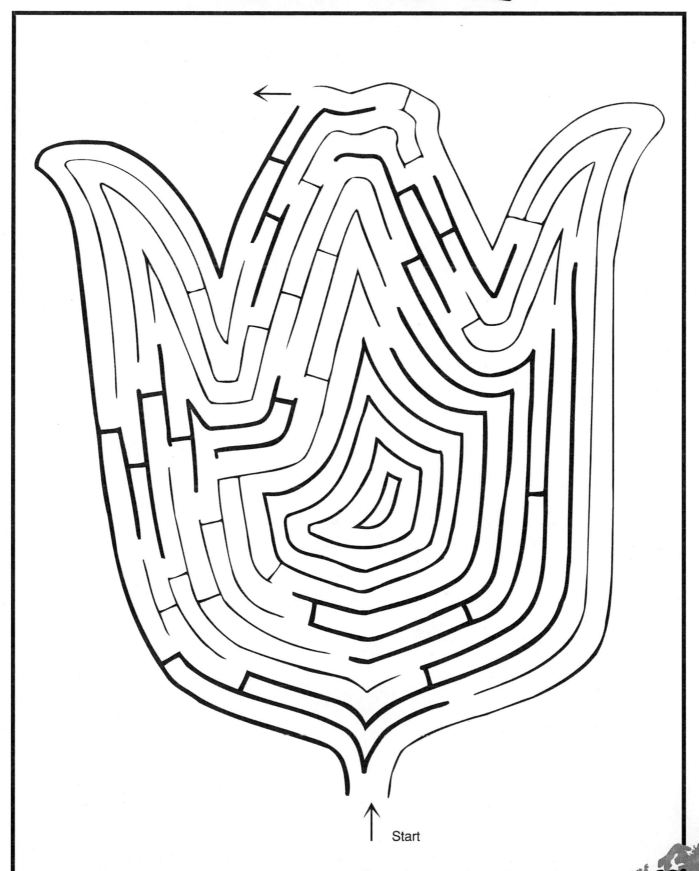

Start

Netherlands

MAZE CRAZE

Find the bee.

Start
Here
↓

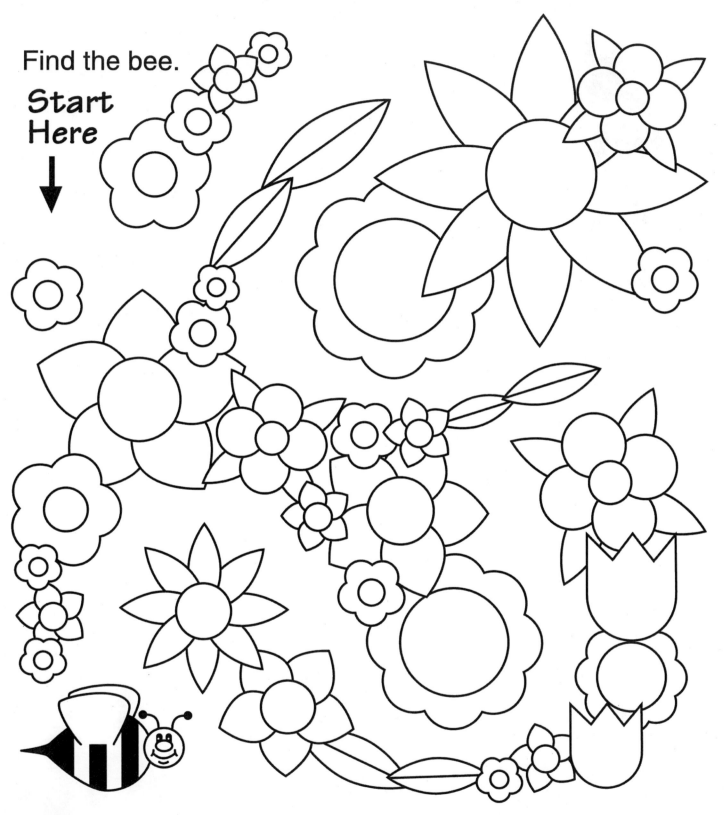

Netherlands

FIND THE TWINS!

WHICH TWO ARE EXACTLY ALIKE?

3

6

2

5

1

4

Spain

Population _____

Capital City _____

Religion _____

Type of Government _____

Currency _____

Language _____

What are the people called? _____

Spain

Spain

Spain, a beautiful, sunny country known for its bullfights, shares the Iberian Peninsula with its neighbor Portugal. The capital city is Madrid.

The flag of Spain is three horizontal stripes of red, yellow, and red with the national coat of arms to the left of center. Red and yellow are the colors of Castille and Aragon, kingdoms ruled and united by King Ferdinand and Queen Isabella.

While Spain is on the continent of Europe, the Carthaginians and Moors of northern Africa helped shape Spain's early history more than the Europeans did. The reason for this is quite simple. Spain is separated from the rest of Europe by the Pyrenees Mountains which at one time made travel between the two quite difficult. The Strait of Gibraltar separates Spain from Africa. At its narrowest point, the Strait is only eight miles wide. This short distance made it possible for the Carthaginians to rule much of Spain for almost two hundred years from around 400 BC. The Moors conquered Spain during the 700s and remained in power for three centuries.

Geography
❑ Peninsula
- *Geography from A to Z,* page 34

History and Biographies
❑ Queen Isabella
- *Queen Isabella I* – Corinn Codye
- *Isabella of Castile* – Joann J. Burch

General References
❑ *Discovering Spain* – Philippa Leahy

❑ *Spain* – Catherine Chambers

❑ *Spain* – Mary Berendes

❑ *Next Stop Spain* – Clare Boast

❑ *Spain* – Kate A. Furlong

❑ *Spanish Food and Drink* – Maria Eugenia D. Pellicer

❑ *Spain* – Kathleen W. Deady

❑ *Spain* – Martin Hintz

❑ *Spain* – Susie Brooks

❑ *Looking at Spain* – Jillian Powell

Literature

- ❑ *Story of Ferdinand* – Munro Leaf
- ❑ *Squash It!* – Eric A. Kimmel
- ❑ *Favorite Fairy Tales Told in Spain* – Virginia Haviland

Language Arts

- ❑ Choose from the Language Arts Suggestions on page 6

Science

- ❑ Bulls: If your library, like ours, does not have books specifically on bulls, look for books on cows or cattle.
  - • *Cows* – Mary Ann McDonald
- ❑ Cork
  - • www.iberianature.com/material/cork_trees_spain.html

Activities

- ❑ Color or make the flag of Spain.
- ❑ Shade the Iberian Peninsula and label the Pyrenees Mountains on a world map.
- ❑ Color or label a map of Spain.
- ❑ Make a Spanish meal from *Eat Your Way Around the World*.
- ❑ Make baked fish, Spanish style.

1½ lbs. fish steaks or fillets	1½ teaspoons salt	2 tablespoons olive oil
¼ teaspoon paprika	¼ teaspoon pepper	Lemon wedges
1 green pepper, cut into rings	1 sliced tomato	2 tablespoons olive oil
1 small onion, sliced	2 tablespoons lemon juice	1 clove garlic, minced

Directions: If fish pieces are large, cut into serving sizes. Arrange fish in ungreased square baking dish; sprinkle with salt, paprika, and pepper. Top with green pepper rings and tomato and onion slices. Mix lemon juice, oil, and garlic; pour over fish. Cover and cook in 375°F oven for 15 minutes. Uncover and cook until fish flakes easily with fork, 10 to 15 minutes longer. Garnish with lemon wedges.

Bible

- ❑ *Story of Ferdinand*
  - • Mark 1:35

- ❑ Bulls
  - • Genesis 41:1–7
  - • Exodus 32
  - • Psalm 22:12
  - • Jeremiah 50:11
  - • Hosea 10:11

Holidays and Celebrations

- ❑ http://en.wikipedia.org/wiki/Public_holidays_in_Spain
- ❑ www.gomadrid.com/practic/public-holidays.html

Travel and Tourism

Tourist Office of Spain
8383 Wilshire Blvd, Suite 960
Beverly Hills, CA 90211

Telephone: 323-658-7188
Email: losangeles@tourspain.es
Website: www.spain.info/us/TourSpain

Flag of Spain

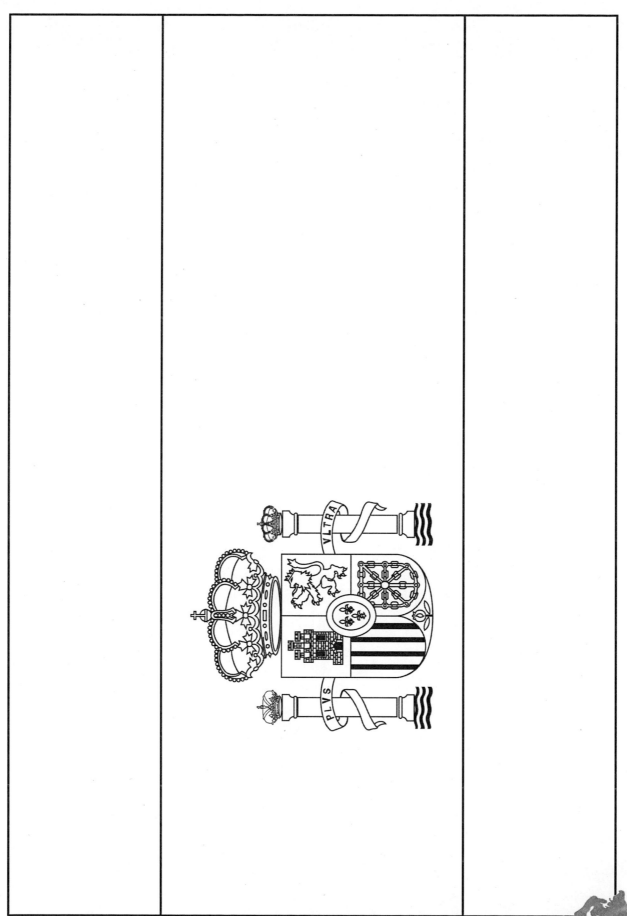

Spain and Portugal

What are people from Spain called? _____

What language do they speak? _____

What are people from Portugal called? _____

What language do they speak? _____

Spain

Word Search

```
q  s  e  u  r  o  p  e  f  g  n  m  g
v  u  o  k  v  c  g  d  y  r  s  p  h
m  d  i  r  u  s  s  i  a  e  g  r  o
v  j  a  k  x  u  p  v  j  a  b  r  l
i  t  a  l  y  b  g  i  j  t  z  p  l
z  o  x  a  b  d  e  a  m  b  g  f  a
l  q  b  w  p  i  r  u  h  r  s  o  n
b  q  e  k  l  a  m  w  z  i  o  a  d
s  p  a  i  n  j  a  i  x  t  j  l  r
l  x  w  f  m  k  n  n  e  a  i  q  y
b  a  c  t  g  j  y  m  o  i  d  r  c
s  f  z  r  j  o  g  t  c  n  u  v  i
a  f  r  a  n  c  e  x  d  e  m  q  r
```

Europe   Holland
France   Italy
Germany   Russia
Great Britain   Spain

111

Europe Review

Europe Review Map

See how many countries you can identify. Write their names on the map.

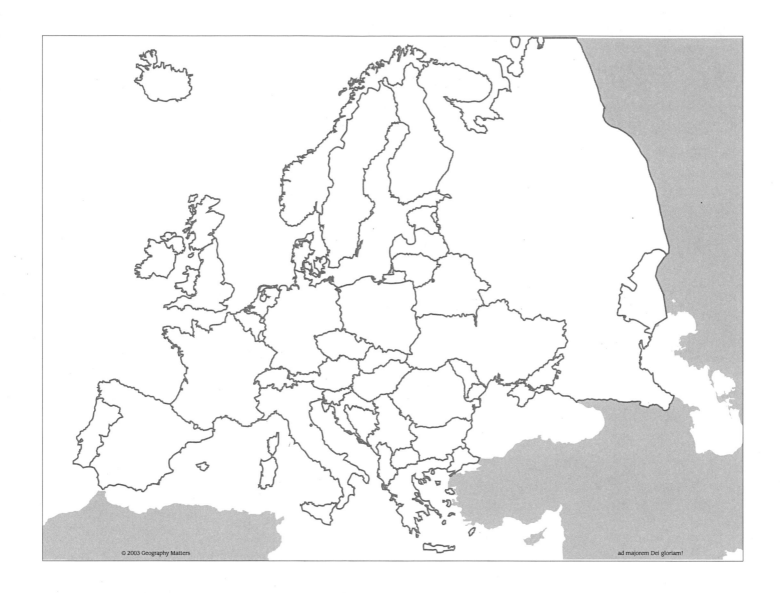

© 2003 Geography Matters

ad majorem Dei gloriam!

Christmas is the most celebrated holiday in the world. Plan on taking the month of December to relax and enjoy learning about the different and wonderful ways Christmas is celebrated around the world. Every country's celebrations vary according to the climate, beliefs, traditions, and folklore of that country. Some countries enjoy some of the same practices and symbols.

A fun activity to consider is setting up a small Christmas tree in your school area. When you study a different country add an ornament to remind your children of the way that country celebrates Christmas.

A very brief description of how 10 different countries celebrate the holiday season follows. Choose the ones you would like to learn more about then check out some of the reference books suggested to find recipes, activities, and music from that individual country.

Japan

Most Japanese are not Christians; therefore, the majority of the Japanese people do not celebrate the religious aspects of the holiday. The Japanese Christmas greeting is "Meri Kurusumasu." Japan has adopted many western Christmas traditions such as exchanging gifts, caroling, and decorating store windows and homes with holly and bells. The Japanese use lanterns, fans, flowers, and dolls to decorate their trees. Hoteiosho is the Japanese Santa Claus. He walks around and observes children with "eyes in the back of his head." If the children are good, he gives them a toy from the bag he carries.

❑ **Activity**: Make small Japanese fans to decorate your international tree.

China

The Chinese New Year is the biggest celebration in China. During this time, the people enjoy gift-giving and fireworks for an entire week. Chains, flowers, and paper lanterns are popular Chinese decorations. Special lanterns shaped like pagodas sometimes show the Holy Family inside. A special gift-bearer, Lan Khoong-Khoong or Nice Old Father, fills the children's stockings with small gifts. Another name for the gift-bearer is Dun Che Lao Ren, the Christmas Old Man.

❑ **Activity**: Make a paper chain for your international tree.

Russia

The Christmas greeting in Russia is "Hristos Razdajetsja." Dyed Maroz, Grandfather Frost, is the Russian Santa Claus. He dresses in a red suit and has a white beard, but delivers gifts on New Year's Day. One traditional gift is a *Matryoshka* doll. The outer doll is opened to reveal smaller dolls nested inside. Another gift-bearer famous in Russia is Babouschka. The legend says that she was visited by the Three Kings, but she was too busy to direct them to the Christ child. Because of her error she is doomed to wander forever and deliver gifts to good children. She pays her visit on Epiphany, January 6. Russian families eat Christmas Eve supper together and decorate their tree with candy, oranges, apples, dolls, fabric, and foil ornaments.

❑ **Activity**: Add oranges or paper dolls to your international tree.

Great Britain

"Happy Christmas" is the English Christmas greeting. Many of the most popular Christmas customs originated in Great Britain. The first Christmas cards were sent in England. Tradition says that boarding school children would send them to their parents. Caroling is another British custom. It is like American caroling, except groups of people sip wassail, a hot punch-like drink, while walking up and down the street. Wassail means "be in good health." This event takes place throughout the twelve days of Christmas (December 25–January 6). Decorations include holly, ivy, and mistletoe. The British also have Christmas "crackers," small circular shapes filled with small prizes that make a cracking sound when ends are pulled open. Christmas dinner often includes twelve or more courses. December 26 is Boxing Day. This is when people rewarded good servants with gifts. Today, community workers often receive this special appreciation.

❑ **Activity**: Add holly, ivy, or mistletoe to your international tree.

France

In France, the season begins on December 5, St. Nicholas Eve. This is one of several days that children receive gifts. The children leave their shoes by the fireplace in hope of receiving special treats. It is believed that France is the first country to begin leaving gifts in the name of St. Nicholas. This custom is popular in many other countries today. Christmas Eve is when parents leave toys, fruit, and candy for the children to find the next day; usually, these are left on the branches of the Christmas tree. Friends and family members give gifts on New Year's Day. The French also made the manger scene popular. Christmas trees are decorated with stars of many different colors and the crèche (manger scene) is the center of the decorations. A few days before Christmas, the family carefully assembles the crèche and decorates it with evergreens and candles. Then they celebrate the birth of Christ by singing carols and rejoicing. Food is very important at the French celebration. Foods like Buche de Noel and Galette des Rois are made this time of year.

❑ **Activity**: Make paper stars of various colors for the international tree.

Italy

Christmas in Italy is a solemn, yet festive, occasion. The first manger scene originated in Italy and was made by St. Francis of Assisi to encourage others to worship Jesus. Italy is credited with the first true Christmas carols. The Italian Christmas begins on the first Sunday of Advent. The nine days before Christmas include bagpipers in the streets, fireworks, bonfires, carols, and lots of lights. The manger scene or *presepio* is set up in homes without baby Jesus; then on Christmas Eve, the figure is passed around and put in the manger with songs and prayers. At 10:00 Christmas Eve mass begins. January 6 is the traditional gift-giving day; however, some families give gifts on Christmas Day as well. These gifts come from Gesu Bambino or Baby Jesus. Christmas Day is a day of church, family, and feasting. The family eats pasta dishes and turkey. On January 6, children receive gifts from La Befana. Legend describes her as a tiny old woman who is dressed in black and rides on a broomstick. Tradition says the Befana was visited by the Three Kings in search of Jesus. They asked her to come along, but she was too busy working. She went to go with them later, but they were already gone. She still searches for them today. She leaves gifts for the good children and ashes or coal for the naughty ones.

❑ **Activity:** Put a manger scene under the international tree.

Germany

"Merry Christmas" in German is *Frohliche Weihnachten*. One of our most important traditions, the Christmas tree, originated in Germany. In the sixteenth century, Martin Luther was the first person to bring an evergreen indoors. While he was outside on Christmas Eve, he was so moved by the tree against the starlight that he cut one down and brought it home. He put lighted candles on it to symbolize the stars over Bethlehem. Families would originally light trees only on Christmas Eve. They decorated them with apples, cookies, candies, and candles. The tradition of the Christmas tree spread to France and England, who are credited with adding the angel on top. There are many gift-bearers in Germany, depending on the various regions. Each one is a helper to Kirst Kindl or Christkindl, the Christ Child. These gifts are brought by a young child dressed in white wearing a crown of candles. In other parts of Germany, Kris Kringle is the giftgiver. He may arrive by mule or white horse. The children leave goodies for him to eat and he, in turn, leaves gifts for the good children. If the children have been bad, then Hans Trapp leaves them switches.

Families in Germany use the advent wreath and light one candle each Sunday. The main celebration is on Christmas Eve, when the Gemans decorate the tree, go to church, eat, sing, and give gifts.

❑ **Activity:** Add dried apples or apple shaped ornaments to the international tree.

Spain

Felices Pascuas is "Merry Christmas" from Spain. Religious celebrations are predominant in mostly Catholic Spain. In Spain, Christmas is celebrated from December 24 to January 6. Public areas are decorated with life-size nativity scenes. Plays depicting the shepherds adoring Jesus are popular events. Spain uses many lights in its decorations. Christmas Eve is the "Good Night" and people fast all day, not eating until after midnight. Bells chime loudly at midnight calling people to midnight mass. After mass the feasting begins. They have *paella* (a rice and seafood dish), fruits, candy, and *chirimoyas* (apple custard). Christmas Day is spent with friends and family. The Three Kings deliver gifts on the eve of January 5. The children leave their shoes out with hopes of finding them filled with toys and treats the next morning. On January 6, there is a parade with kings and animals up and down the streets.

❑ **Activity:** Add bells to your international tree.

Mexico

Feliz Navidad is the Christmas greeting in Mexico. Like Spain, Mexico is mostly Catholic. The Processions of Las Posadas are very important in Mexico. These processions symbolize the travels of Mary and Joseph to Bethlehem. People divide into two groups, the innkeepers and the travelers. Stopping places are chosen ahead of time. At each stop, the travelers are denied entry until the last stop, where the group is invited in for eating and celebrating. These processions occur December 16–24. The final celebration includes fried sugar tortillas, hot chocolate, and a piñata for the children to break open. After nine evenings of celebrating, Christmas Day is a quiet family time with feasting and reflection. On January 6, the children receive their gifts from the Three Kings. They leave their shoes out to be filled with gifts and treats. The poinsettia, the traditional Christmas plant, is native to Mexico, where it grows wild in damp areas. In 1829, the U.S. ambassador to Mexico brought the plant home to the U.S.

❑ **Activity:** Play "innkeepers and travelers" using different rooms of your home.
Add silk poinsettias to the international tree or place a poinsettia plant beside tree.

Nigeria

Almost half of Nigerians are Christians; therefore, many Christian customs are practiced in Nigeria. Large church pageants are performed and used to spread the gospel to non-believers. Instead of gifts, Nigerians often give food on Christmas Day. They make extra of their favorite dishes and send portions to their friends and neighbors. Christmas afternoon, children go from house to house singing carols anticipating candy or cookies in return. Music is important in Nigeria, and the drum and other instruments are used extensively in Christmas celebrations.

❑ **Activity:** Have children create their own Christmas pageant using lots of music.

Christmas Around the World

History and Biographies

❑ St. Nicholas

For centuries St. Nicholas has been associated with Christmas and gifts. His name, originally from the Latin, Sanctus Nicolaus, has had various forms, including the German, Sankt Nikolaus, Dutch Sinter Klaas, finally becoming our modern "Santa Claus." Although he is regarded as a myth, there actually was a real St. Nicholas, an early Christian who lived during the fourth century.

Nicholas, the only child of wealthy Christian parents, was born at the end of the third century at Patara, a port in the province of Lycia in Asia Minor. From early childhood his mother taught him the Scriptures. When both parents died during an epidemic, they left the young boy in possession of all their wealth.

Young Nicholas dedicated his life to God's service and moved to Myra, the chief city of his province. One of Nicholas's best characteristics was his unsurpassed generosity. In his youth he had met many people who were oppressed by poverty. As a result, he often went out in disguise and distributed presents, especially to children. Stories of Nicholas's kindness and liberality soon spread. As a result, when unexpected gifts were received, he was given credit as the donor.

General References

❑ *Holiday Cooking Around the World* (Lerner Publications)

❑ *Christmas Cooking Around the World* – Susan Purdy

❑ *A Christmas Companion* – Maria Robbins and Jim Charlton

❑ *Christmas in (name of country)* series (Worldbook)

❑ *The Whole Christmas Catalog for Kids* – Louise Betts Egan

❑ *Christmas Crafts and Customs Around the World* – Virginia Fowler

❑ *Celebrating Christmas Around the World* – Herbert Werneke

❑ *A Christmas Companion: Recipes, Traditions, and Customs from Around the World* – James Charlton

❑ *Silent Night: Its Story and Song* – Margaret Hodges

❑ *Christmas Around the World* – Mary D. Lankford

❑ *Merry Christmas Everywhere* – Arlene Erlbach

❑ www.californiamall.com/holidaytraditions/home.htm

❑ www.soon.org.uk/country/christmas.htm

❑ http://christmas-world.freeservers.com//index.html

❑ www.pastrywiz.com/cookies/index.html

❑ www.santas.net/aroundtheworld.htm

Literature

❑ *Ellis Island Christmas* – Maxinne Rhea Leighton

❑ *The Bird's Christmas Carol* – Kate Douglas Wiggin

❑ *The Christmas Tree Ship* – Jeanette Winter

❑ *A Christmas Tree in the White House* – Gary Hines

❑ *Christmas Tree Memories* – Aliki

❑ *Tree of Cranes* – Allen Say

- ❑ *Jotham's Journey* – Arnold Ytreeide
- ❑ *Papa's Christmas Gift* – Cheryl Harness
- ❑ *An Amish Christmas* – Richard Ammon
- ❑ *A Candle for Christmas* – Jean Speare
- ❑ *A Northern Nativity: Christmas Dreams of a Prairie Boy* – William Kurulek
- ❑ *The Best Christmas Pageant Ever* – Barbara Robinson
- ❑ *Too Many Tamales* – Gary Soto
- ❑ *The Legend of the Poinsettia* – Tomie dePaola

Science

- ❑ Deer and Reindeer
  - *Reindeer* – Emery and Durga Bernhard
  - *Reindeer* (A New True Book) – Emilie U. Lepthien
  - *Deer, Moose, Elk, and Caribou* – Deborah Hodge
  - *All About Deer* – Jim Arnosky
  - *Never Grab a Deer by the Ear* – Colleen Stanley Bare
  - *White-Tailed Deer* (A New True Book) – Joan Kalbacken
  - *Little Caribou* – Sarah Fox-Davies
  - www.enchantedlearning.com/subjects/mammals/deer/Reindeerprintout.shtml

Activities

- ❑ Make lots of Christmas crafts.
- ❑ Learn Christmas carols and sing them for others.
- ❑ Go to http://coloring-page.net/activity/pages/dot-10.html for a Christmas tree maze.
- ❑ Go to www.familycorner.com/dir/Family/Kids/Coloring_Pages/Activities/Mazes/ for two Christmas mazes.
- ❑ Go to www.enchantedlearning.com/crafts/christmas/handtree/index.shtml for a hand print tree craft.
- ❑ Go to www.familycorner.com/dir/Family/Kids/Coloring_Pages/Holidays/Christmas/ for coloring pages.

Bible

- ❑ Luke 2:1–40
- ❑ Deer
  - Genesis 49:21
  - 2 Samuel 2:18
  - 2 Samuel 22:33–34
  - Psalm 18:30–33
  - Psalm 29:9
  - Psalm 42:1
  - Isaiah 35:6
  - Habakkuk 3:19

MAZE CRAZE

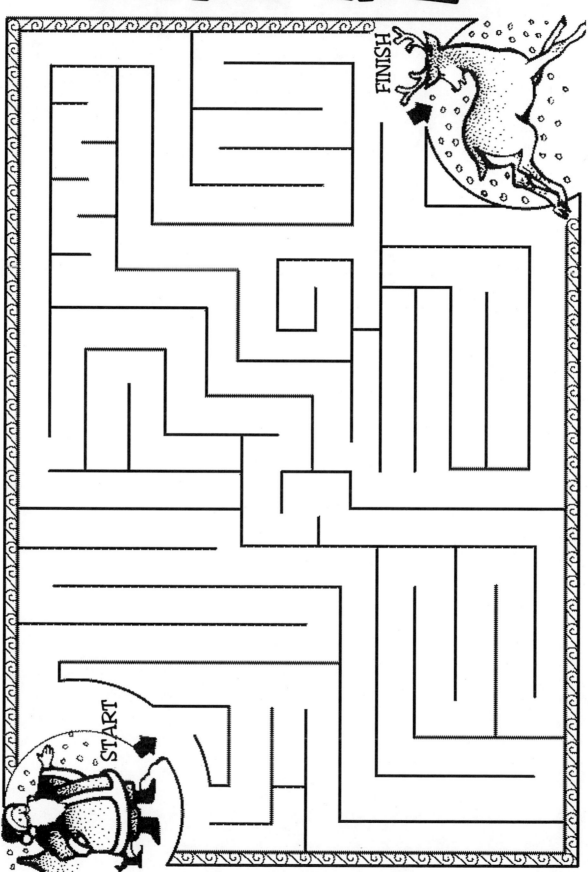

FINISH

START

Christmas Around the World

The Poles

The North Pole lies in the area known as the Arctic Circle. This bitterly cold region includes the northern parts of Asia, Europe, and North America.

The South Pole is on the continent of Antarctica. While several countries have laid claim to Antarctica, the international community recognizes none of these claims. The continent's only inhabitants are scientists from around the world.

120

The Poles

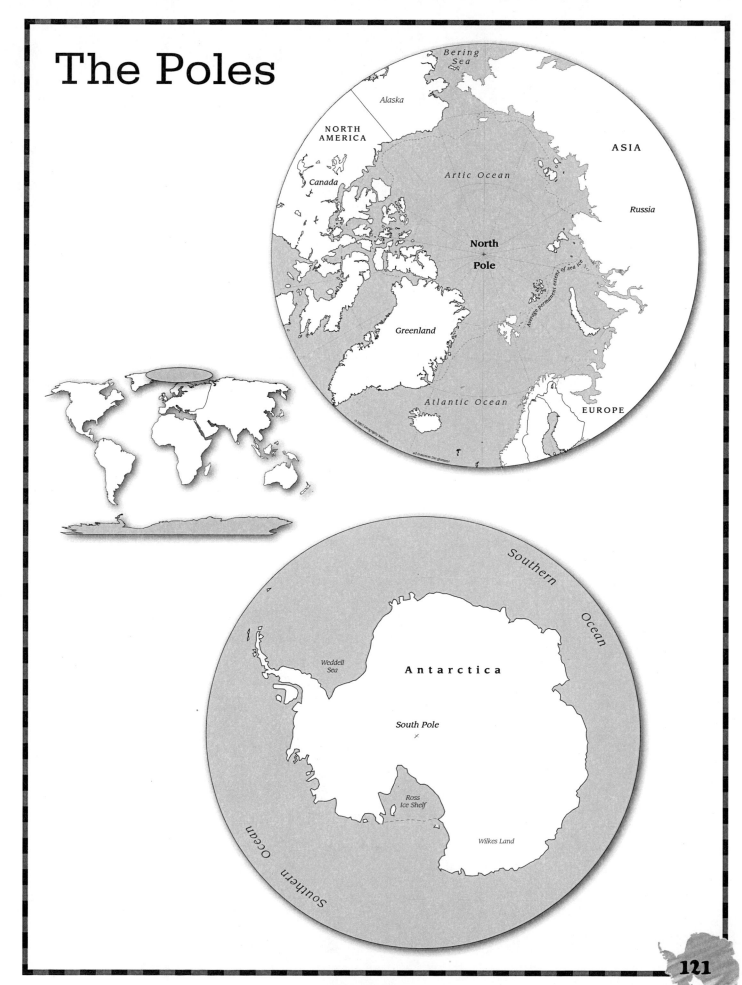

North Pole map labels: Bering Sea, Alaska, NORTH AMERICA, Canada, Artic Ocean, ASIA, Russia, North Pole, Greenland, Average permanent extent of sea ice, Atlantic Ocean, EUROPE

South Pole map labels: Southern Ocean, Weddell Sea, Antarctica, South Pole, Ross Ice Shelf, Wilkes Land, Southern Ocean

Antarctica

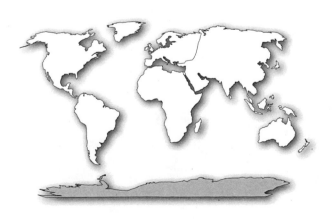

122

Antarctica

Antarctica

At twice the size of the United States, Antarctica is the fifth largest continent. Its position at the South Pole along with its elevation makes it the coldest place on earth. Although Antarctica receives only about five inches of snow each year, it is so cold that the snow never melts and continues to accumulate.

Seven countries claim territory in Antarctica, but their claims are not recognized by the rest of the world. The Antarctic Treaty is an international agreement to reserve the continent for scientific study. Research stations have been set up for that purpose.

Geography
- ❑ Iceberg
    - *Geography from A to Z,* page 24
- ❑ Floe
- ❑ Ice sheet

History and Biographies
- ❑ Roald Amundsen
    - *Usborne Book of Explorers*, page 41
    - www.enchantedlearning.com/explorers/page/a/amundsen.shtml
- ❑ Ernest Shackleton
    - *Sea of Ice: Wreck of the Endurance* – Monica Kulling
    - *Shackleton's Antarctic Adventure* – video/DVD by Image Entertainment
    - www.enchantedlearning.com/explorers/page/s/shackleton.shtml
- ❑ Sir James Ross
    - www.enchantedlearning.com/explorers/page/r/ross.shtml
- ❑ Robert Scott
    - www.enchantedlearning.com/explorers/page/s/scott.shtml

General References
- ❑ *Windows on Nature: Animals of the Polar Region* – Debora Burr
- ❑ *Polar Wildlife* – Joshua Morris
- ❑ *A for Antarctica* – Jonathan Chester
- ❑ *Antarctica* (A True Book) – David Petersen
- ❑ *Polar Lands* – Christopher Green
- ❑ *Take a Trip to Antarctic* – Keith Lye
- ❑ *Antarctica* (A New True Book) – Lynn M. Stone

- *Polar Exploration* – Martyn Bramwell
- *Our Father's World,* pages 72–75
- *Hooray for Antarctica!* – April Pulley Sayre
- *Antarctica* – Katie Bagley
- *Antarctica* – Allan Fowler

Literature

- "The Strange Case of Moody, Watch, and Spy" – *Your Story Hour* (Album 7 Patterns of Destiny)

Language Arts

- Choose from the Language Arts Suggestions on page 6.
- Write a story or keep a journal as if you were a scientist doing research in Antarctica.

Science

- Penguin
  - *Zoo Guide*, page 119
  - *Aquarium Guide*, page 183
  - *Plenty of Penguins* – Sonia W. Black
  - http://kids.nationalgeographic.com/Animals/CreatureFeature/Emperor-penguin (reference to evolution)
  - http://kids.nationalgeographic.com/Animals/CreatureFeature/Adelie-penguin
- Weddell Seal
  - www.enchantedlearning.com/subjects/mammals/pinniped/Weddellsealprintout.shtml

Activities

- The Antarctic is "owned" internationally and does not have a flag of its own. Let the child design a flag.
- Label the Antarctic and South Pole on a world map.
- For penguin craft ideas, go to
  - www.dltk-kids.com/animals/measypenguin.html
  - www.dltk-kids.com/animals/mpenguin.html
  - http://familycrafts.about.com/cs/penguins/l/blpbpeng1.htm
- For printable penguin pages, go to
  - www.coloring.ws/penguins1.htm
  - www.enchantedlearning.com
- Make a Weddell seal out of modeling clay.

Bible

- Snow
  - Job 24:19
  - Job 37:6
  - Job 38:22–23
  - Psalm 147:15–16
  - Isaiah 1:18–20
  - Isaiah 55:10
- Ice
  - Job 6:15–16
  - Job 38:30

Word Search

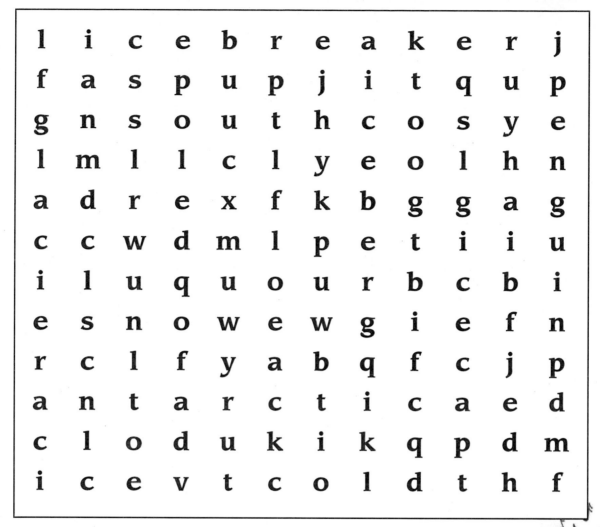

l i c e b r e a k e r j
f a s p u p j i t q u p
g n s o u t h c o s y e
l m l l c l y e o l h n
a d r e x f k b g g a g
c c w d m l p e t i i u
i l u q u o u r b c b i
e s n o w e w g i e f n
r c l f y a b q f c j p
a n t a r c t i c a e d
c l o d u k i k q p d m
i c e v t c o l d t h f

Antarctica   icebreaker
cold   icecap
floe   penguin
glacier   pole
ice   snow
iceberg   south

The Arctic

This is God's view from the top of the world.

What 3 continents have land near the North Pole?

1. _____

2. _____

3. _____

126

The Arctic

The Arctic

Portions of three continents lie within the bitterly cold region north of the Arctic Circle known as the Arctic. In the center of this region is the North Pole. While this area is bitterly cold, it is not the coldest place on earth. That distinction goes to the Arctic's polar opposite, the Antarctic.

The Arctic isn't always covered with snow. Ninety percent of the land within the Arctic Circle is free of snow and ice during the summer months. Berries, flowers, and even vegetables will grow in some areas.

During the long, cold winter, there is at least one day when the sun does not shine at all on the Arctic. The closer you are to the North Pole, the longer the period with no sun. During the short, cool summer, there is at least one day when the sun does not set. And just opposite of the winter, the closer you are to the North Pole in the summer, the longer the sun shines.

Geography

- ❑ Crevasse
    - *Geography from A to Z,* page 14
- ❑ Glacier
    - *Geography from A to Z,* page 20
- ❑ Ice Cap

History and Biographies

- ❑ Robert Peary and Matthew Henson
    - *Matthew Henson: Arctic Explorer* – Jeri Ferris
    - www.enchantedlearning.com/explorers/page/p/peary.shtml
- ❑ Wilfred Grenfell
    - *Wilfred Grenfell: The Arctic Adventurer* – Linda Finlayson
- ❑ Vilhjalmur Stefansson
    - *Vilhjalmur Stefansson: Young Arctic Explorer* – Hortense Myers and Ruth Barnett
    - www.enchantedlearning.com/explorers/page/s/stefansson.shtml

General References

- ❑ *Windows on Nature: Animals of the Polar Region*
- ❑ *Polar Wildlife* – Joshua Morris
- ❑ *Polar Lands* – Christopher Green
- ❑ *Arctic Babies* – Kathy Darling
- ❑ *Arctic Lands* edited by Henry Pluckrose
- ❑ *Polar Exploration* – Martyn Bramwell

❑ *Arctic Spring* – Sue Vyner

❑ *Arctic Kingdom: Life At The Edge* – National Geographic Video

Literature

❑ *Little Polar Bear, Take Me Home* – Hans de Beer

Language Arts

❑ Choose from the Language Arts Suggestions on page 6.

❑ Make a desktop project of an igloo. Refer to the *Big Book of Books and Activities*, page 42.

❑ Make a poster or brochure advertising an arctic zoo. Make sure to include pictures (cut from magazines or drawn by hand) and descriptions of all animals that will be seen in this zoo.

Science

❑ Wolverine
  - *Zoo Guide*, page 103
  - www.enchantedlearning.com/subjects/mammals/weasel/Mustelids.shtml
  - www.enchantedlearning.com/subjects/mammals/weasel/Wolverineprintout.shtml
  - http://kids.nationalgeographic.com/Animals/CreatureFeature/Wolverines
  - http://animals.nationalgeographic.com/animals/mammals/wolverine.html

❑ Arctic fox
  - *Zoo Guide*, page 15
  - *Arctic Foxes* – Downs Matthews
  - *Pocket Factfiles: Mammals*, pages 34–35
  - www.enchantedlearning.com/subjects/mammals/fox/Arcticfoxprintout.shtml
  - http://animals.nationalgeographic.com/animals/mammals/arctic-fox.html

❑ Seal
  - *Aquarium Guide*, page 201
  - *Cousteau Society: Seals*
  - *Harp Seal Pups* – Downs Matthews
  - *Pocket Factfiles: Mammals*, pages 92–97
  - www.enchantedlearning.com/subjects/mammals/pinniped/Harpsealprintout.shtml
  - www.enchantedlearning.com/subjects/mammals/pinniped/Northernfurseal.shtml
  - http://animals.nationalgeographic.com/animals/mammals/harp-seal.html

❑ Orca (Killer Whale)
  - *Aquarium Guide*, page 203
  - *Considering God's Creation*, lesson 26b
  - *Killer Whales* – Dorothy Hinshaw Patent
  - *Killer Whales* – Mark Carwardine
  - *Pocket Factfiles: Mammals*, pages 70–71
  - www.enchantedlearning.com/subjects/whales/species/Orca.shtml
  - http://kids.nationalgeographic.com/Animals/CreatureFeature/Orca
  - http://animals.nationalgeographic.com/animals/mammals/killer-whale.html

❑ Snowy Owl
- *Zoo Guide*, page 151
- *Snowy Owl at Home on the Tundra*
- *Snowy Owl* – Baby Animal Stories
- www.enchantedlearning.com/subjects/birds/printouts/Snowyowlprintout.shtml
- www.enchantedlearning.com/crafts/animals/owl/
- http://kids.nationalgeographic.com/Animals/CreatureFeature/Snowy-owl
- http://animals.nationalgeographic.com/animals/birds/snowy-owl.html

❑ Polar Bear
- *Zoo Guide*, page 75
- *Polar Bears* – Marcia S. Freeman
- *Polar Bear Cubs* – Downs Matthews
- *Polar Bear Alert* – National Geographic Explorer Video
- *Pocket Factfiles: Mammals,* pages 42–43
- *Magnificent Mammals,* page 48
- www.enchantedlearning.com/subjects/mammals/bear/Polarbearcoloring.shtml
- www.enchantedlearning.com/subjects/mammals/bear/polarbearbook/
- http://kids.nationalgeographic.com/Animals/CreatureFeature/Polar-bear
- http://animals.nationalgeographic.com/animals/mammals/polar-bear.html

Activities

❑ Make a model igloo.

3 cups flour   1½ cups salt   1½ cup water

Directions: In a bowl, mix flour, salt, and half the water. Gradually add the remaining water. Knead until a ball is formed.

Press dough into two ice cube trays. Freeze at least two hours. Remove blocks.

On a piece of paper, draw or trace a circle 4 inches across. Fit the blocks on their sides along the circle with the small ends facing inward.

Igloos are built on a spiral. Use a ruler to cut the first two blocks at a slant, forming a ramp. Continue to place blocks around the circle and up the ramp in a spiral. Trim blocks to fit as they close in to form a dome.

When the dome is finished, use trimmings to fill in the gaps. Cut a door at the base.

To harden, bake in a 125°F oven.

❑ Label the Arctic Circle and the North Pole on a world map.

❑ Go to www.familycorner.com/family/kids/color/activities/maze_igloo.shtml for an igloo maze.

Bible

❑ Refer to Bible references for Antarctica.

Word Search

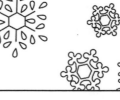

```
w o l v e r i n e s t
b h d z p w l l r n s
a f r s e a l v f o n
r o m o f f u e o w l
c x m p g c b a c y f
t u n o r t h p o y d
i y z l e x r v r r i
c p s e b m s i c f g
t h p o t b w z a o l
p o l a r b e a r n o
j y m q t u n d r a o
```

Arctic
fox
igloo
north
orca
owl

polar bear
pole
seal
snowy
tundra
wolverine

The Arctic

MAZE CRAZE

FINISH

North America

North America is the third largest continent and has the fourth largest population. It is bordered by the Atlantic Ocean on the east and the Pacific Ocean on the west. The highest point is Mt. McKinley in Alaska (20,320 ft.). The lowest point is at Death Valley, California, where the elevation is 282 ft. below sea level. North America's vast natural resources and rich mineral reserves have produced two of the largest manufacturing countries in the world.

North America

Color each country you study.

Artic Ocean

USA

Greenland

Canada

Labrador Sea

Hudson
Bay

Lake
Superior
Lake
Huron
Lake
Michigan
Lake
Ontario

United States of America

Atlantic Ocean

Mexico

Gulf
of
Mexico

Bahamas

Cuba

Dom. Rep.

Jamacia

Haiti

Belize
Guatemala
Honduras
El Salvador
Nicaragua

Caribbean Sea

Pacific Ocean

Costa Rica

Panama

© 2003 Geography Matters

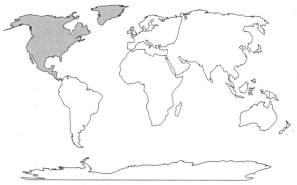

133

Canada

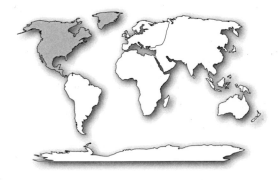

134

Population _____

Capital City _____

Religion _____

Type of Government _____

Currency _____

Language _____

What are the people called? _____

Canada

Canada

Canada is the world's second largest country. With its majestic mountains, crystal-clear lakes, wind-swept prairies, and thick forests, Canada is a land of great, natural beauty. Canada's name comes from kanata, the Huron word meaning "to the village." The capital city is Ottawa.

The flag of Canada is vertical red, white, and red bands with a red maple leaf in the center. The maple leaf is Canada's national symbol.

Canada and the United States have long been good friends. On the border between the two countries is a stone marker with these words, "To God in His Glory, we two nations dedicate this garden and pledge ourselves that as long as men shall live, we will not take up arms against one another."

Geography
❑ St. Lawrence River

❑ Hudson Bay

❑ Bay
- *Geography from A to Z,* page 9

History and Biographies
❑ Royal Canadian Mounted Police (Mounties)

The Mounties are as much a symbol of Canada as the maple leaf. The Mounties were originally recruited in 1873 to prevent bloodshed between whiskey traders and Native People in the Northwest Territories. Riding horseback, they brought law and order to the expanding Canadian frontier.

The Mounties' red coats were a symbol of peace, the color was chosen because the Native People equated red with justice and fair dealing. The broad-brimmed hats were adopted by 1900 because they offered protection from the sun. Today, the Mounties wear the red coat for dress and ceremonial occasions, including parades.

❑ Henry Hudson
- *Henry Hudson Explorer of the North* – Dorothea J. Snow
- *The Voyages of Henry Hudson* – Eugene Rachlis
- www.enchantedlearning.com/explorers/page/h/hudson.shtml

❑ Jacques Cartier
- *Jacques Cartier and the Exploration of Canada* – Daniel E. Harmon
- *Cartier: Finder of the St. Lawrence* – Ronald Syme

General References

- ❑ *North America* (A True Book) – David Petersen
- ❑ *A is for the Americas* – Cynthia Chin-Lee and Terri de la Pena
- ❑ *Our Father's World,* pages 8–30
- ❑ *Take a Trip to Canada* – Keith Lye
- ❑ *Count Your Way Through Canada* – Jim Haskins
- ❑ *Children Just Like Me,* page 23
- ❑ *Canada* – Michael Dahl
- ❑ *Canada* – Shirley W. Gray

Literature

- ❑ *Missionary Stories with the Millers,* chapters 28–29
- ❑ *I Know an Old Lady Who Swallowed a Fly* retold by Nadine Bernard Westcott
- ❑ *Very Last First Time* – Jan Andrews
- ❑ *Chester's Barn* – Lindee Climo
- ❑ *A Regular Rolling Noah* – George Ella Lyon
- ❑ *Prairie Boys Winter* – William Kurelek
- ❑ *The Flight of the Union* – Tehla White
- ❑ *The Fiddler of the Northern Lights* – Natalie Kinsey-Warnock

Language Arts

- ❑ Choose from the Language Arts Suggestions on page 6.
- ❑ Write a play about life on a farm or life in the Royal Canadian Mounted Police.
- ❑ Use the words on the marker between Canada and the United States as copy work.

Science

- ❑ Moose
  - *Pocket Factfiles: Mammals,* pages 148–149
  - *Magnificent Mammals,* page 44
  - *Zoo Guide,* page 67
  - www.enchantedlearning.com/subjects/mammals/deer/
    Mooseprintout.shtml
  - http://animals.nationalgeographic.com/animals/mammals/moose.html
- ❑ *Considering God's Creation,* lesson 23
- ❑ Play "Into the Forest" by Ampersand Press.
- ❑ If you read *Very Last First Time,* discuss dressing for weather conditions.
- ❑ If you read *Chester's Barn,* check out some books on different farm animals from the library or read ones already on your shelf.
  - *Farm Animals* (A New True Book) – Karen Jacobsen
  - www.enchantedlearning.com/themes/farmanimals.shtml
- ❑ If you read *A Regular Rolling Noah,* continue with study of farm animals and/or read a book about trains.

Activities

❑ Color or make the flag of Canada.

❑ Color or label a map of Canada.

❑ Label the St. Lawrence River and the Hudson Bay on a world map.

❑ Play or watch hockey.

❑ Celebrate Canada's winter climate with a snowball fight. If no snow is available, use wadded paper or foam balls.

❑ Maple Mousse Recipe (This recipe is from the Province of Quebec.)

1 envelope unflavored gelatin	3 eggs, separated
¼ cup cold water	1 cup whipping cream
1 cup maple syrup	1 T maple extract

Sprinkle gelatin over cold water and set aside.

Combine maple syrup and egg yolks in top of double boiler; cook over simmering water, stirring constantly, until slightly thickened, about 8 minutes.

Remove from heat; add softened gelatin and stir until melted.

Transfer to large bowl, let cool, then chill, stirring occasionally until maple custard thickens and is the consistency of unbeaten egg whites, about 20 minutes.

In large bowl, beat egg whites until stiff but not dry. In a separate bowl, whip cream until stiff. Stir about 1 cup egg whites into maple custard, whisk until smooth. Fold in remaining egg whites, whipped cream and liqueur.

Spoon mousse into 6 individual serving dishes or a 4-cup glass bowl. Cover and chill for 3 to 4 hours.

❑ Make a totem pole like the Native Americans of Canada's northwest coast.

Use empty cans of the same size and cover them with colored paper. Decorate each can using paint, markers, or crayons. Stack cans on top of one another and hold together with glue.

❑ Make Habitant Pea Soup.

This is a French-Canadian dish adapted from the traditional food carried by voyageurs on their long trips.

1¼ lbs. dried peas	2 diced onions
½ lb. salt pork	3 bay leaves
11 cups water	1 tsp. salt
½ cup chopped celery	1 tsp. savory
¼ cup chopped parsley	

Directions: Wash and drain peas. Put them in a soup pot with water. Boil for 2 minutes; remove from heat and cool 2 hours. Add remaining ingredients. Bring soup to a boil again; reduce heat and simmer 2 hours.

❑ Make a Canadian meal from *Eat Your Way Around the World.*

137

❑ Make snowshoes.
- Have child stand on poster board or cardboard.
- Trace around each foot. Measure an oval 6 inches larger than the outline of each foot.
- Cut out cardboard or poster board.
- Have the child stand on the cut out boards.
- Make markings for three to five holes on each side of each foot.
- Punch holes at markings.
- Lace the holes with a long piece of yarn or twine.
- Tie in place over child's shoes.

❑ Make a Canadian forest scene.
- To make tree trunks, cut 1 inch wide strips of brown construction paper.
- Glue onto white construction paper.
- Tear small pieces of green tissue paper or construction paper.
- Glue onto white construction paper in an overlapping pattern to make the leaves on the trees.

❑ Make a maple leaf mobile – option 1.
- Color copies of the maple leaf pattern on page 141 red or use them as a pattern to trace onto red paper or photocopy onto red paper.
- Cut out leaves.
- Poke a small hole in the lop of each leaf.
- Thread string through the hole and tie onto a clothes hanger at varying lengths.

❑ Make a maple leaf mobile – option 2.
- Color four copies of the medium size maple leaf pattern on page 129 red. Cut out.
- Trace a CD onto white paper four times. Cut out the four circles.
- Glue a red maple leaf to the center of each white circle. Allow to dry.
- Gently fold each circle in half so that the fold runs through the leaf vertically.
- Match the spines of two circles side-by-side. Glue edges together. Repeat with other two circles.
- Allow to dry.
- Tie a knot on one end of an 18″ piece of yarn.
- Glue the two halves together with the yarn running through the middle. Allow to dry.

❑ Go to http://coloring-page.net/trains.html for train coloring pages.

❑ Go to www.crayola.com/free-coloring-pages/print/canada-parliament-hill-coloring-page/ for a coloring page of the Canadian Parliament.

❑ Go to www.crayola.com/free-coloring-pages/print/poppies-to-remember-coloring-page/ for a Remembrance Day craft.

❑ Go to www.crayola.com/free-coloring-pages/print/canada-leaf-wreath-coloring-page/ for a Canadian leaf wreath.

❑ Go to www.coloring.ws/canada.htm for printable coloring pages.

Bible

- ❑ *Missionary Stories with the Millers*, chapter 28
  - Joshua 1:5
  - Psalm 46:1
  - 1 Thessalonians 5:18
  - 2 Thessalonians 3:3
- ❑ *Missionary Stories with the Millers*, chapter 29
  - Acts 27
- ❑ *Very Last First Time*
  - Psalm 27:1
  - Isaiah 41:10
- ❑ *A Prairie Boy's Winter*
  - Ecclesiastes 3:1–8
- ❑ Farm Animals
  - Genesis 30:31–43
  - Exodus 26:7
  - Matthew 7:6
  - Mark 5:11–13
  - Luke 15:11–32
  - 2 Peter 2:22

Holidays and Celebrations

- ❑ www.pch.gc.ca/progs/cpsc-ccsp/jfa-ha/index_e.cfm

Travel and Tourism

Canadian Tourism Commission
8th Floor West, 235 Queen Street
Ottawa, ON K1A 0H6

Telephone: 613-946-1000

Website: www.keepexploring.ca

Flag of Canada

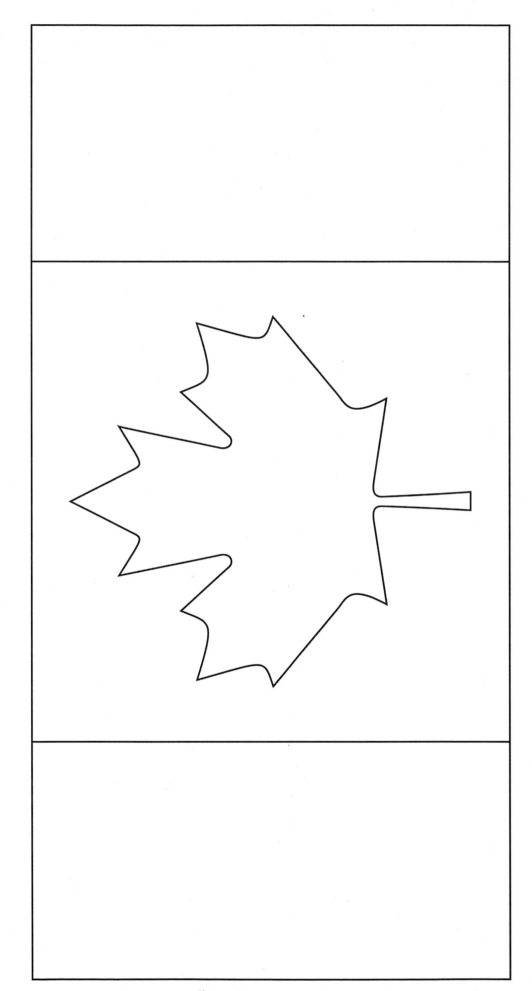

140

Canada

Maple Leaf Pattern

Stars

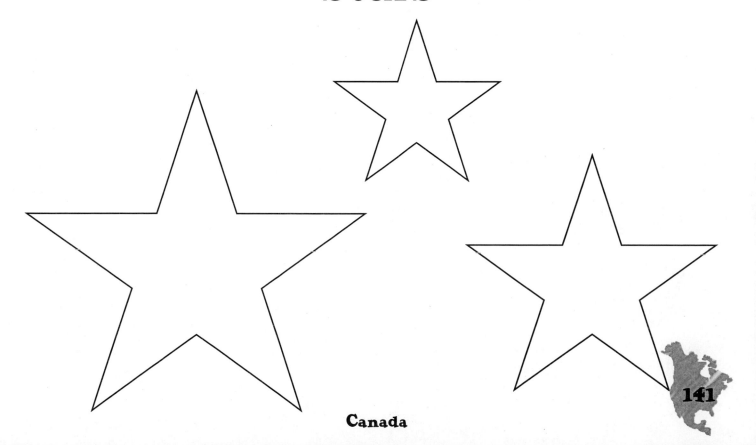

Canada

141

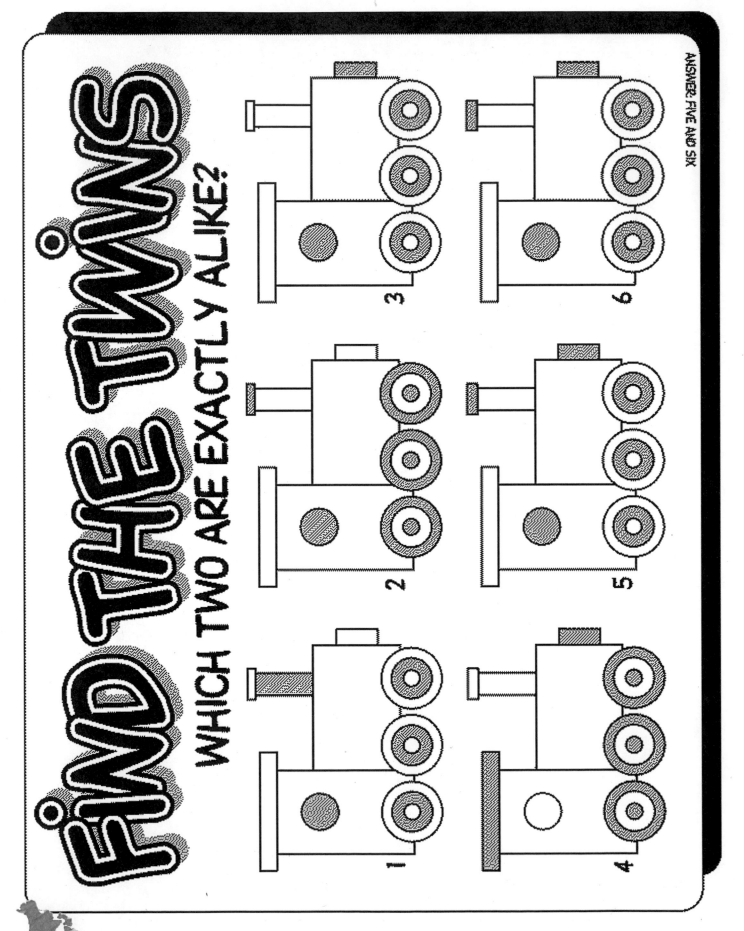

FIND THE TWINS

WHICH TWO ARE EXACTLY ALIKE?

1

2

3

4

5

6

142

Canada

MAZE CRAZE

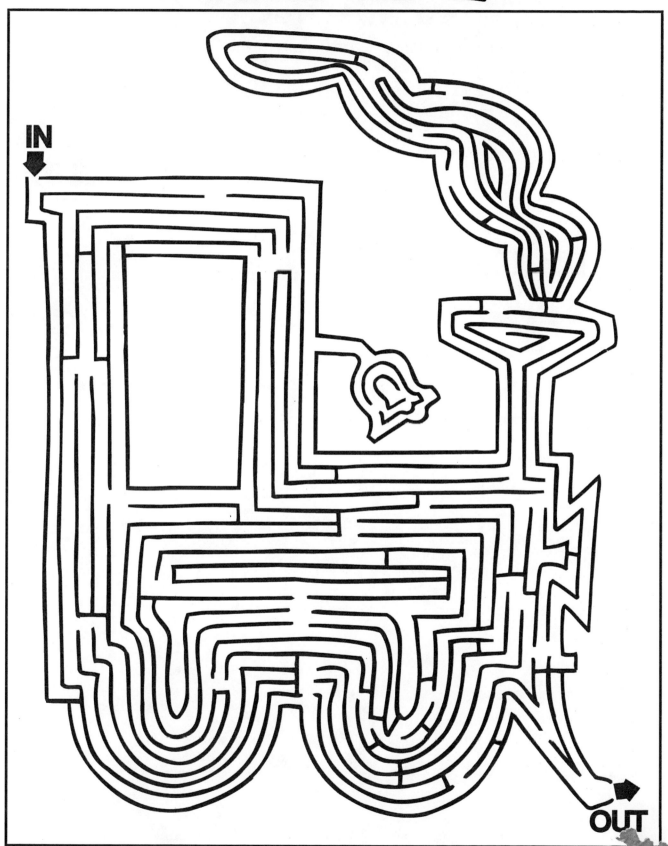

IN

OUT

143

Canada

Crossword Puzzle

Across
2 neigh
4 meow
6 quack-quack
9 cock-a-doodle-doo
10 oink-oink

Down
1 cluck-cluck
3 baa
4 moo
5 gobble-gobble
7 woof-woof

Canada

Word Search

```
c  g  d  u  c  k  n  n  p  g
o  p  o  c  u  w  m  p  i  h
w  o  g  o  o  s  e  i  g  g
s  c  f  f  i  y  a  r  o  l
w  h  o  r  s  e  q  o  b  s
z  i  v  q  z  a  y  o  n  h
g  c  m  u  g  h  a  s  t  e
c  k  s  s  o  u  r  t  m  e
c  e  a  x  a  i  w  e  k  p
s  n  f  t  t  w  d  r  f  t
```

chicken	goat	pig
cow	goose	rooster
duck	horse	sheep

145

Canada

The United States of America

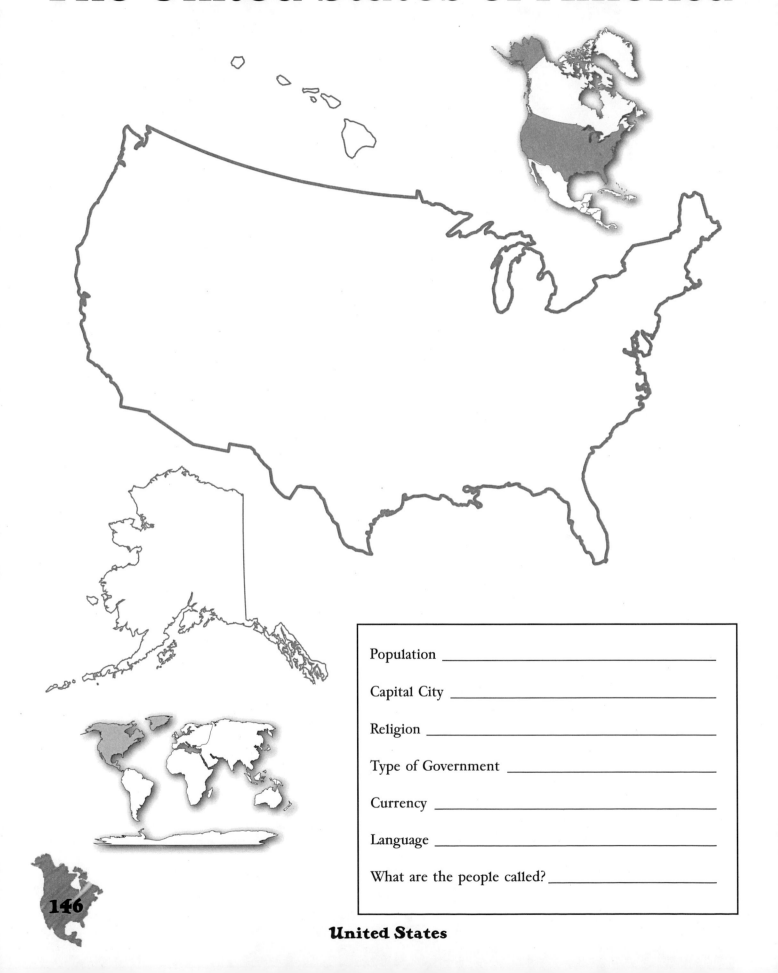

Population _____

Capital City _____

Religion _____

Type of Government _____

Currency _____

Language _____

What are the people called? _____

146

United States

Covering the entire midsection of North America, along with Alaska in northwest North America and Hawaii in the Pacific Ocean, the United States is the fourth largest country in the world. Often referred to as a "melting pot," the people of the United States trace their heritage to all other parts of the world. The land is as varied as its people. From coastal beaches and lowlands to towering mountains with rolling plains and dry deserts in between, the United States is as beautiful as it is large.

The flag of the United States is known as the "Stars and Stripes." The thirteen red and white stripes symbolize the thirteen original colonies. Each of the fifty states is represented by a star on the field of blue in the upper left corner of the flag. When a new state joined the Union, a new star was added to the flag the following July 4th, Independence Day.

The United States was founded on the principles of freedom and liberty. These freedoms are guaranteed in the Constitution, the oldest governing document in the world. At 4,440 words, the Constitution of the United States is also the shortest written constitution in the world.

Geography

❑ Rocky Mountains
- *Rocky Mountain National Park* – David Petersen

❑ Mountain Range
- *Geography from A to Z,* page 31

History and Biographies

There are many more historical figures than can be covered in this section. We chose to cover presidents.

❑ George Washington
- *George Washington* – Garnet Jackson
- *Buttons for General Washington* – Peter and Connie Roop
- *Meet George Washington* – Heilbrendt
- *A Picture Book of George Washington* – David A. Adler
- *Phoebe the Spy* – Judith Berry Griffin
- *Profiles from History* Volume 3, page 19

❑ Thomas Jefferson
- *Profiles from History* Volume 1, page 123
- *Meet Thomas Jefferson* – Marvin Barrett
- *Young Thomas Jefferson* – Francene Sabin
- *A Picture Book of Thomas Jefferson* – David A. Adler

- ❑ Abraham Lincoln
    - *Abe Lincoln's Hat* – Martha Brenner
    - *Just a Few Words, Mr. Lincoln* – Jean Fritz
    - *Meet Abraham Lincoln* – Carey
    - *A Picture Book of Abraham Lincoln* – David A. Adler
    - *Profiles from History* Volume 3, page 75
- ❑ Barrack Obama (or current president)
    - www.whitehouse.gov
- ❑ Native American Indians
    - *Indians* (A New True Book) – Teri Martini
- ❑ American Flag
    - *Our Flag* – Leslie Waller
    - *The American Flag* (A True Book) – Patricia Ryon Quiri
    - *Red, White, and Blue* – John Herman
    - *The Star Spangled Banner* – Peter Spier

General References

- ❑ *Welcome to the Sea of Sand* – Jane Yolen
- ❑ *Yosemite National Park* (A New True Book) – David Petersen
- ❑ *Children Just Like Me,* pages 18–22
- ❑ *Mount Rushmore* – Thomas S. Owens
- ❑ *Alaska* – Joyce Johnston
- ❑ *First Facts About the United States* – David L. Steinecker
- ❑ *America's Forests* – Frank Staub

Literature

- ❑ *Missionary Stories with the Millers*, chapters 22 and 25, as well as the Introduction
- ❑ *Great for God (Heaven's Heroes)*, chapters 6, 10, 15, and 21
- ❑ The Cranberry series by Wende and Harry Devlin are wonderful books set in New England. There are several titles in the series – *Cranberry Thanksgiving, Cranberry Valentine, Cranberry Easter,* etc. Choose the one that is set in the season you are currently experiencing. Plan ahead and make the recipe at the end of the book.
- ❑ *When I Was Young in the Mountains* – Cynthia Rylant
- ❑ *Lentil* – Robert McClosky
- ❑ *Yankee Doodle* – Edward Bangs
- ❑ *The Story of the Statue of Liberty* – Betsy and Giulio Maestro
- ❑ *Copper Lady* – Alice Ross
- ❑ *Maybelle, the Cable Car* – Virginia Lee Burton
- ❑ *The Snow Walker* – Margaret K. Wetterer
- ❑ *Chang's Paper Pony* – Eleanor Coerr
- ❑ *My Great Aunt Arizona* – Gloria Houston
- ❑ *Only Opal* – Barbara Cooney

- ❑ *First Flight* – George Shea
- ❑ *Countdown to Flight* – Steve Englehart
- ❑ *They Were Strong and Good* – Robert Lawson
- ❑ *Oxcart Man* – Barbara Cooney
- ❑ *With a Whoop and a Holler* – Nancy Van Laan

Language Arts

- ❑ Choose from the Language Arts Suggestions on page 6.

- ❑ Make up a travel brochure for your state. Include interesting facts, pictures, historical sites, and other interesting things that would attract people to your state.

- ❑ Make a bound book with pictures and/or drawings of some of the animals in America. Have the child put them in alphabetical order for practice. Refer to the *Big Book of Books and Activities*, page 50.

Science

- ❑ Buffalo
  - *Buffalo* (A New True Book) – Emilie U. Lepthien
  - *Considering God's Creation*, lesson 26a
  - *Pocket Factfiles: Mammals*, pages 154–157
  - *Magnificent Mammals*, page 10
  - www.enchantedlearning.com/subjects/mammals/bison/Bisoncoloring.shtml
  - http://animals.nationalgeographic.com/animals/mammals/american-bison.html

- ❑ Rabbit
  - *Zoo Guide*, page 79
  - *Cottontail Rabbits* – Kristin Ellerbusch Gallagher
  - *Diary of a Rabbit* – Lilo Hess
  - *Rabbits, Rabbits, and More Rabbits* – Gail Gibbons
  - *Pocket Factfiles: Mammals*, pages 210–211
  - www.enchantedlearning.com/themes/rabbit.shtml
  - http://animals.nationalgeographic.com/animals/mammals/cottontail-rabbit.html

- ❑ Beaver
  - *Zoo Guide*, page 23
  - *Beavers* – Deborah Hodge
  - *Pocket Factfiles: Mammals*, pages 172–173
  - *Magnificent Mammals*, page 14
  - www.enchantedlearning.com/subjects/mammals/Beaver.shtml
  - www.coloring.ws/beaver.htm
  - http://animals.nationalgeographic.com/animals/mammals/beaver.html

- ❑ Otter
  - *Zoo Guide*, page 85
  - *Sea Otters* – Evelyn Shaw
  - *Playful Slider* – Barbara Juster Esbensen
  - *Oopsie Otter* – Suzanne Tate
  - *Sea Otters* – Sophie Lockwood
  - www.enchantedlearning.com/subjects/mammals/weasel/Riverotterprintout.shtml

- http://kids.nationalgeographic.com/Animals/CreatureFeature/River-otter
- http://animals.nationalgeographic.com/animals/mammals/giant-river-otter.html

❑ Squirrel
- *The Squirrel and the Nut* (God is Good Series) – Rod and Staff
- www.enchantedlearning.com/subjects/mammals/rodent/Squirrelprintout.shtml
- www.coloring.ws/squirrel.htm
- http://animals.nationalgeographic.com/animals/mammals/squirrel.html

❑ Skunk
- *Zoo Guide,* page 91
- *Magnificent Mammals,* page 58
- *Skunks* – Sandra Lee
- *Pocket Factfiles: Mammals,* pages 60–61
- www.enchantedlearning.com/subjects/mammals/skunk/Skunkcoloring.shtml
- http://animals.nationalgeographic.com/animals/mammals/skunk.html

❑ Raccoon
- *Pocket Factfiles: Mammals,* pages 46–47
- *Magnificent Mammals,* page 54
- *Baby Raccoon* – Beth Spanjian
- *Clever Raccoons* – Kristin L. Nelson
- www.enchantedlearning.com/crafts/puppets/paperbag/index.shtml
- www.enchantedlearning.com/subjects/mammals/raccoon/Raccoonprintout.shtml
- http://animals.nationalgeographic.com/animals/mammals/raccoon.html

❑ Porcupine
- *Zoo Guide,* page 71
- *Pocket Factfiles: Mammals,* pages 200–201
- *Magnificent Mammals,* page 50
- www.enchantedlearning.com/subjects/mammals/rodent/Porcupineprintout.shtml
- http://animals.nationalgeographic.com/animals/mammals/porcupine.html

❑ Cougar
- *Zoo Guide,* page 165
- *Pocket Factfiles: Mammals,* pages 24–25
- *Baby Cougar* – Beth Spanjian
- www.enchantedlearning.com/subjects/mammals/cats/cougar/Cougarprintout.shtml

❑ Prairie Dog
- *Zoo Guide,* page 77
- *Prairie Dog at Home on the Range* – Sarah Toast
- *Baby Animal Stories* – "Prairie Dog"
- www.enchantedlearning.com/subjects/mammals/rodent/Prairiedogprintout.shtml
- http://animals.nationalgeographic.com/animals/mammals/prairie-dog.html

❑ Manatee
- *Zoo Guide,* page 61
- *Aquarium Guide,* page 205
- *I Wonder if Sea Cows Give Milk* – Annabelle Donati
- *Manatee Winter* – Kathleen Weidner Zoehfeld
- *A Safe Home for Manatees* – Priscilla Belz Jenkins

- *A Manatee Morning* – Jim Arnosky
- www.enchantedlearning.com/subjects/mammals/manatee/index.shtml
- http://kids.nationalgeographic.com/Animals/CreatureFeature/West-indian-manatee
- http://animals.nationalgeographic.com/animals/mammals/manatee.html

❑ General Animal Books
- *Armadillos Sleep in Dugouts and Other Places Animals Live* – Pam Munoz Ryan
- *Animal Babies* – illustrated by Fiammetta Dogi
- *God Made the Animals* – God is Good Series by Rod and Staff
- *Animal Homes* – First Little Golden Book
- *Big Tracks, Little Tracks* – Millicent E. Selsam
- *America: Land of Wildlife* – Karen Jensen
- *Wonders of the Forest* – Francene Sabin

Activities

❑ Color or make the flag of the United States.

❑ Color or label a map of the United States.

❑ Label the Rocky Mountains on a world map.

❑ Put together a puzzle of the United States.

We prefer the puzzles that have each state as an individual piece. Most teacher supply stores carry them as well as Timberdoodle (360-426-0672 or www.timberdoodle.com) and Hands On and Beyond (1-888-20-LEARN or www.HandsOnAndBeyond.com).

❑ Try recipes from regions of the country other than your own. *Eat Your Way Through the USA* by Loree´ Pettit provides recipes for preparing a complete meal with ingredients or dishes associated with each state.

❑ Listen to *The Stories of Foster and Sousa* (Music Masters Series).

❑ Make American Flag graham crackers.

Ingredients: graham crackers, white chocolate chips (for the stars), tubes of red, white, and blue frosting or white frosting with red and blue sugar sprinkles for stripes and blue field.

❑ Listen to the "Star Spangled Banner" and other patriotic music. Wee Sing America (www.weesing.com) is a good source of patriotic music for children.

❑ Find out the origin of your state's name.

❑ Many communities have wildlife refuges or nature centers. Visit one in your area.

❑ Make a star mobile – option 1.
- Color copies of the star pattern on page 141 or use them as a pattern to trace onto red, white and blue paper or photocopy onto red, white and blue paper.
- Cut out stars.
- Poke a small hole in the top of each star.
- Thread string through the hole and tie onto a clothes hanger at varying lengths.

❑ Make a star mobile – option 2.
- Copy or trace the largest star pattern on page 141 onto white paper four times. Cut out four stars.
- Trace a CD onto red paper two times and onto blue paper two times. Cut out the four circles.
- Glue a white star to the center of each red and blue circle. Allow to dry.
- Gently fold each circle in half so that the fold runs vertically through the tip of each star.

- Match the spines of two circles side-by-side. Glue edges together. Repeat with other two circles.
- Allow to dry.
- Tie a knot on one end of an 18″ piece of yarn.
- Glue the two halves together with the yarn running through the middle. Allow to dry.

❑ Go to www.dltk-kids.com/usa/musaposter.html for printable coloring pages.

Bible

❑ *Missionary Stories with the Millers*, chapter 22
- Galatians 6:2

❑ *Missionary Stories with the Millers*, chapter 25
- Matthew 13:1–9, 18–23
- Matthew 25:13
- Luke 12:20

❑ *When I Was Young in the Mountains*
- Matthew 3:13–17
- Matthew 28:19–20
- John 1:32–34
- John 3:16
- Acts 8:26–40

❑ *Lentil*
- Genesis 4:2–15
- Proverbs 18:16
- John 21:20–23

❑ *Maybelle, the Cable Car*
- Deuteronomy 32:7

❑ *Chang's Paper Pony*
- Leviticus 19:35–36
- Deuteronomy 25:15
- Proverbs 11:1
- Proverbs 17:5
- Revelation 21:21b

❑ *The Snow Walker*
- Job 29:15–16
- Matthew 25:35a

❑ *They Were Strong and Good*
- Genesis 12:3b
- Genesis 25:12–26
- Matthew 1:1–17

❑ *Oxcart Man*
- Proverbs 6:6–8
- Acts 20:34
- Ephesians 4:28b

❑ Rabbit
- Leviticus 11:6

Holidays and Celebrations

❑ www.english-zone.com/holidays/

❑ www.mdusd.k12.ca.us/sequoiamiddle/calendar/traditions.html

Travel and Tourism

The United States does not have a central tourism office. Each of the 50 states has their own individual offices. Go to www.usa.gov/Citizen/Topics/Travel_Tourism/State_Tourism.shtml for a listing of the contact information for the state offices.

Flag of the United States of America

United States

153

U.S.A. Time Zones

Alaska

Pacific

Mountain

Central

Eastern

© 2003 Geography Matters

ad majorem Dei gloriam!

Color your state.

What are the people from your state called? _____

What is your state nickname? _____

In which time zone do you live? _____

154

United States

MAZE

Find the capital of Kansas.

Start Here

Topeka

U.S.A.

Crossword Puzzle

Across

6 The longest river in the U.S.
8 This man is credited with discovering America.
11 The Aloha State.
12 This President ended slavery.
14 The Peach State.
15 The Bluegrass State.

Down

1 The Grand Canyon State.
2 The first President.
3 Old Dominion.
4 The Show-me State.
5 The Lone Star State.
7 The first state to join the Union.
9 The number of states in the U.S.
10 The Sunshine State.
13 The Garden State.

United States

MAZE CRAZE

START

FINISH

157

United States

Word Search

```
x m n e a t w n p l x u a
w a s h i n g t o n d c m
o x c w k e y j g x u q e
s t r i p e s m l e o s r
t c u h j t w f b k h c i
a v z z r d h g l x t r c
r x a f e x i m u p w j a
s f g h d p t w e l n v f
v f c s k s e o u x o x t
g i d f r e e d o m a o z
f f a i e v j j h c p o z
s t a t e s v x x m l r f
f y g g c n l i b e r t y
```

America   stars
blue   states
fifty   stripes
freedom   Washington DC
liberty   white
red

United States

Word Search

p	z	t	p	a	m	a	n	a	t	e	e
r	h	b	e	a	v	e	r	i	l	c	z
a	f	a	z	k	e	s	o	b	b	i	o
i	x	y	b	f	o	q	m	u	y	q	t
r	d	g	b	j	e	u	y	f	e	r	t
i	q	b	m	q	p	i	q	f	r	a	e
e	c	o	u	g	a	r	w	a	j	c	r
d	t	h	m	f	b	r	l	l	l	c	x
o	s	k	u	n	k	e	r	o	t	o	d
g	o	l	x	o	t	l	w	u	l	o	s
t	r	f	p	o	r	c	u	p	i	n	e
r	a	b	b	i	t	t	r	z	p	j	h

beaver   prairie dog
buffalo   rabbit
cougar   raccoon
manatee   skunk
otter   squirrel
porcupine

159

Mexico

160

Population _____

Capital City _____

Religion _____

Type of Government _____

Currency _____

Language _____

What are the people called? _____

Mexico

Mexico

Mexico borders the United States from California to Texas. A large portion of the boundary between the United States and Mexico is formed by the Rio Grande. Made up of high mountains, tropical forests, and dry deserts, the landscape and climate of Mexico can change drastically in a very short distance. The capital is Mexico City.

The flag of Mexico is a green, white, and red tricolor with the Mexican coat of arms in the center. Green represents independence. White stands for religion. Red symbolizes unity.

For centuries, ancient civilizations thrived in what is now Mexico. The Spanish conquered the area in the early 16th century and remained in control for almost three hundred years. In 1821, the Spanish controlled government was overthrown and Mexico gained independence.

Geography
- ❑ Gulf
  - *Geography from A to Z,* page 22
- ❑ Gulf of Mexico

History and Biographies
- ❑ *Charro: The Mexican Cowboy* – George Ancona
- ❑ Benito Juarez
  - *Benito Juarez: Hero of Modern Mexico* – Rae Bains
  - *Benito Juarez* – Jan Gleiter
- ❑ Hernando Cortes
  - *Hernando Cortes and the Conquest of Mexico* – Gina De Angelis
- ❑ Mexican Independence
  - www.enchantedlearning.com/history/mexico/independence/
- ❑ Pancho Villa

General References
- ❑ *Our Father's World,* pages 105–111
- ❑ *A Family in Mexico* – Tom Moran
- ❑ *Count Your Way Through Mexico* – J. Haskins
- ❑ *Passport to Mexico* – C. Irizarry
- ❑ *Mexico* (A New True Book) – K. Jocobsen
- ❑ *Mexico* – Kate A. Furlong

- ❑ *Inside Mexico* – Ian James
- ❑ *Mexico* (A True Book) – Ann Heinrichs
- ❑ *Children Just Like Me,* pages 16–17
- ❑ *Mexico* – Shirley W. Gray
- ❑ *Mexico* – Michael Dahl
- ❑ *Mexico ABCs* – Sarah Heiman

Literature

- ❑ *Hill of Fire* – Thomas P. Lewis
- ❑ *Happy Days with Pablo and Juanita* – Evelyn Hege (Rod and Staff)
- ❑ *Missionary Stories with the Millers*, chapters 10 and 16
- ❑ *The Tale of Rabbit and Coyote* – Tony Johnston
- ❑ *Doctor Coyote* – John Bierhorst
- ❑ *Huevos Rancheros* – Stefan Czernecki
- ❑ *Cactus Soup* – Eric A. Kimmel
- ❑ *Domitila* – Jewell Reinhart Coburn
- ❑ *Borreguita and the Coyote* – Verna Aardema
- ❑ *Nursery Tales Around the World* – Judy Sierra, "The Ram in the Chile Patch"

Language Arts

- ❑ Choose from the Language Arts Suggestions on page 6.
- ❑ Make a question and answer book on Volcanoes. Refer to the *Big Book of Books and Activities,* page 98.

Science

- ❑ Volcano
  - *Volcanoes* – Franklyn M. Branley
  - *Volcanoes! Mountains of Fire* – Eric Arnold
  - *Why Do Volcanoes Blow Their Tops?* – Melvin and Gilda Berger
  - *Volcanoes* (A New True Book) – Helen J. Challand
  - *Usborne Internet-linked Science Encyclopedia,* page 182–183
  - www.enchantedlearning.com/subjects/volcano/

Activities

- ❑ Color the flag of Mexico.
- ❑ Color or label a map of Mexico.
- ❑ Label the Gulf of Mexico on a world map.
- ❑ Use clay to make an adobe house. Let the house dry in the sun.
- ❑ Make a Mexican meal from *Eat Your Way Around the World.*
- ❑ Learn to count to ten in Spanish.

uno – one	seis – six
dos – two	siete – seven
tres – three	ocho – eight
cuatro – four	nueve – nine
cinco – five	dies – ten

- ❑ Go to www.crayola.com/free-coloring-pages/print/mexican-festival-flags-coloring-page/ for a Mexican festival flag craft.
- ❑ Go to www.enchantedlearning.com/crafts/flowers/tissueflower/ for a tissue paper craft.
- ❑ Make Huevos Rancheros.

6 6-inch corn tortillas	2 T oil
½ cup chopped onion	1 clove garlic, minced
3 large tomatoes, peeled and chopped	¼ tsp salt
4 oz can of green chiles, undrained	6 eggs
½ cup grated cheddar or Monterey Jack cheese	

Directions: Preheat oven to 350°F.

Fry tortillas, one at a time, in hot oil, 5 seconds on each side or just until softened. Drain tortillas on paper towels. Line a 9"×13" baking dish with tortillas, set aside.

Sauté onion and garlic until crisp-tender. Add tomatoes, chiles, and salt. Simmer, uncovered, 10 minutes, stirring occasionally.

Pour mixture over tortillas. Make 6 indentations in tomato mixture, and break an egg into each. Cover and bake at 350°F for 25 minutes. Sprinkle with grated cheese and bake an additional 2 minutes.

Bible

- ❑ Volcano
  - Psalm 104:32
- ❑ Donkey
  - Genesis 22:3
  - Job 6:5
  - Job 39:5–8
  - Proverbs 26:3
  - Matthew 21:1–7
- ❑ *Missionary Stories with the Millers*, chapter 10
  - Acts 16:16–40

Holidays and Celebrations

- ❑ *Cinco de Mayo* – Alice K. Flanagan
- ❑ *Cinco de Mayo* – Lola M. Schaefer
- ❑ *Mexican Independence Day and Cinco de Mayo* – Dianne M. MacMillan
- ❑ *Cinco de Mayo: Yesterday and Today* – Maria Christina Urrutia
- ❑ www.mexonline.com/holiday.htm
- ❑ http://en.wikipedia.org/wiki/Holidays_and_celebrations_in_Mexico

Travel and Tourism

Mexico Tourism Board
21 East 63rd Street, 2nd Floor
New York, NY 10021

Telephone: 1-800-44-MEXICO (toll-free in USA)
Email: newyork@visitmexico.com
Website: www.visitmexico.com

Flag of Mexico

164

Mexico

Crossword Puzzle

Across

3 Spanish for eight.
5 Spanish for six.
8 Spanish for four.
9 Spanish for ten.

Down

1 Spanish for three.
2 Spanish for one.
4 Spanish for five.
6 Spanish for seven.
7 Spanish for nine.
9 Spanish for two.

Word Search

```
p  s  o  m  b  r  e  r  e  r  o  g  i  h  g  v
s  f  e  v  z  a  p  i  n  a  t  a  r  k
e  q  w  s  e  n  o  r  b  t  y  x  a  c
n  h  b  o  f  m  p  a  m  i  g  o  c  y
o  x  u  r  i  o  m  i  j  m  t  q  i  x
r  f  r  n  e  u  e  y  c  n  o  u  a  n
i  y  r  z  s  s  x  i  a  q  s  z  s  f
t  h  o  x  t  d  i  s  c  k  t  l  n  c
a  a  p  i  a  j  c  g  t  d  a  i  i  h
v  t  a  c  o  f  o  c  u  p  d  y  k  a
r  j  o  c  x  g  s  f  s  z  a  h  m  r
v  o  l  c  a  n  o  i  e  w  m  w  q  r
d  m  g  v  s  w  n  b  u  r  r  i  t  o
e  n  c  h  i  l  a  d  a  y  p  h  q  e
```

amigo	enchilada	senorita
burrito	fiesta	sombrero
burro	gracias	taco
cactus	Mexico	tostada
charro	pinata	volcano
	senor	

North America Review Map

See how many countries you can identify. Write their names on the map.

© 2003 Geography Matters

ad majorem Dei gloriam!

South America

South America is the fourth largest continent with the fifth largest population. The west coast is dominated by the mighty Andes Mountains, which run the length of the continent from Columbia to Tierra del Fuego. Both the highest point and lowest point in South American are in Argentina. Cerro Acancagua is 22,831 ft. high and the lowest point, Salinas Chicas, is 138 ft. below sea level. South America is home to the Amazon River, which is surrounded by the world's largest rain forest.

South America

Color each country you study.

Caribbean Sea

Venezuela

Guyana

Suriname

French Guiana

Colombia

Ecuador

Peru

Brazil

Bolivia

Atlantic Ocean

Paraguay

Chile

Uruguay

Argentina

Falkland Islands

© 2003 Geography Matters   ad majorem Dei gloriam!

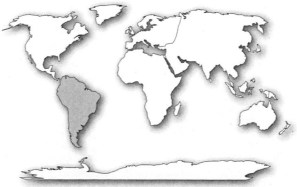

South America

South America

South America

General References

- ❑ *Our Father's World,* pages 54–61
- ❑ *South America* (A True Book) – David Petersen
- ❑ *Magellan and the Exploration of South America* – Colin Hynson
- ❑ *South American Animals* – Caroline Arnold
- ❑ *South America, Surprise!* – April Pulley Sayre
- ❑ *South America* – Mike Graf

Literature

- ❑ *Kitten in the Well* – Rod and Staff
- ❑ *Capyboppy* – Bill Peet
- ❑ *Great for God* (*Heaven's Heroes*), chapters 5 and 20
- ❑ *Missionary Stories with the Millers,* chapter 11

Science

- ❑ Birds
  - *Usborne First Nature: Birds*
  - *How Does a Bird Fly?* – Usborne Starting Point Science
  - *How Do Birds Find Their Way?* – Roma Gans
  - *When Birds Change Their Feathers* – Roma Gans
  - *A Nest Full of Eggs* – Priscilla Belz Jenkins
  - *The Bird Book* – Laura Storms
  - *Considering God's Creation,* lesson 18
  - Build a birdbath, birdhouse, or feeding tray.
  - http://coloring-page.net/activity/pages/dot-8.html
  - http://coloring-page.net/pages/parrot5.html
  - *Usborne Internet-linked Science Encyclopedia,* page 306

Bible

- ❑ *Capyboppy*
  - Proverbs 27:4
  - Proverbs 29:1
  - Proverbs 28:13–14
  - I Corinthians 3:3
  - Galatians 5:26
- ❑ Birds
  - Genesis 1:21
  - Genesis 1:30
  - Genesis 2:19
  - Genesis 8:6–12
  - Deuteronomy 4:17
  - Psalm 124:7–8
  - Proverbs 27:8
  - Ecclesiastes 12:4
- ❑ *Missionary Stories with the Millers,* chapter 11
  - Acts 9:1–31

MAZE CRAZE

Start

South America

MAZE CRAZE

Help the bird
into the house.

Start
Here →

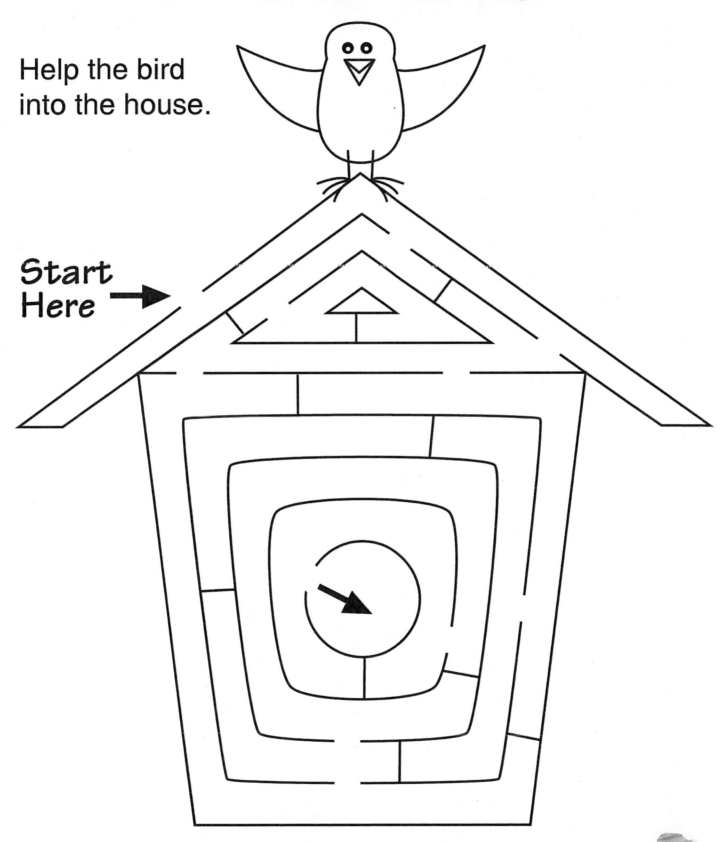

South America

Word Search

```
f  o  r  e  s  t  n  s  j  f  v
z  p  a  v  a  d  t  t  f  w  e
p  f  i  u  b  r  a  z  i  l  n
e  m  n  v  m  z  b  n  a  c  e
r  d  t  i  x  y  m  h  r  j  z
u  k  s  o  u  t  h  m  a  s  u
v  a  m  e  r  i  c  a  c  x  e
p  o  w  z  j  q  h  g  y  z  l
y  y  g  z  k  c  a  v  t  f  a
p  a  r  g  e  n  t  i  n  a  m
v  o  e  n  f  x  z  p  w  r  l
```

America   Peru
Argentina   rain
Brazil   South
forest   Venezuela

South America

Brazil

176

Population _____

Capital City _____

Religion _____

Type of Government _____

Currency _____

Language _____

What are the people called? _____

Brazil

Brazil

Covering almost half of South America, Brazil shares a border with ten countries. Its population is larger than all other South American countries combined. Brasilia is the capital city.

The flag of Brazil is a yellow lozenge on a green field with a blue orb in the center. A band across the center is inscribed with the country's motto which translates, "Order and Progress." Green represents the rain forest. Yellow symbolizes mineral wealth. The twenty-seven stars represent the number of states in Brazil.

The world's second longest river, the Amazon, flows eastward across northern Brazil. The Amazon is also the widest river in the world. Sixty million gallons of water each second flow from the Amazon into the Atlantic Ocean. Surrounding its banks is the world's largest rain forest. Approximately twenty-five percent of all known plants can be found in the Amazon Rainforest.

Geography
- ❑ Amazon River
- ❑ Jungle
  - *Geography from A to Z,* page 26

General References
- ❑ *Brazil* (A True Book) – Ann Heinrichs
- ❑ *Count Your Way Through Brazil* – Jim Haskins
- ❑ *A Family in Brazil* – Olivia Bennett
- ❑ *Children Just Like Me*, pages 14–15
- ❑ *Brazil* – Marion Morrison
- ❑ *Rain Forest Adventures* – Horace Banner (available from Timberdoodle)
- ❑ *Brazil* – Shirley W. Gray
- ❑ *Brazil* – Michael Dahl
- ❑ *Brazil* – Elma Schemenauer

Literature
- ❑ *So Say the Little Monkeys* – Nancy Van Laan

Language Arts
- ❑ Choose from the Language Arts Suggestions on page 6.
- ❑ Write a report on the rain forests in Brazil.
- ❑ Read about life in Brazil. Write a story about the typical day in the life of a Brazilian child.

Science

- ❑ Tamarin
  - www.zooatlanta.org/home/animals/mammals/golden_lion_tamarin
  - http://www.enchantedlearning.com/subjects/mammals/tamarin/Goldenliontamarin.shtml
  - http://en.wikipedia.org/wiki/Tamarin
- ❑ Tapir
  - http://www.enchantedlearning.com/subjects/mammals/tapir/Tapirprintout.shtml
  - http://animals.nationalgeographic.com/animals/mammals/tapir.html(Reference to millions of years)
- ❑ Capybara
  - http://nationalzoo.si.edu/Animals/Amazonia/Facts/capybarafacts.cfm
  - http://www.enchantedlearning.com/subjects/mammals/rodent/Capybaraprintout.shtml
  - http://en.wikipedia.org/wiki/Capybara
- ❑ Piranha
  - *Aquarium Guide,* page 61
  - http://www.enchantedlearning.com/subjects/fish/printouts/Piranhaprintout.shtml
- ❑ Rain Forest
  - *Wonders of the Rain Forest* – Janet Craig
  - *Rain Forests* – Anna O'Mara
  - *One Day in the Tropical Rain Forest* – Jean Craighead George
  - www.enchantedlearning.com/subjects/rainforest/Allabout.shtml

Activities

- ❑ Color the flag of Brazil.
- ❑ Color or label a map of Brazil.
- ❑ Label the Amazon River on a world map. Shade in the Amazon Rain Forest.
- ❑ Play soccer, the national sport.
- ❑ Play *ferol bola.*

  To make your own *ferol bola* game, all you need are two wooden paddles (the actual ones are slightly larger than ping pong paddles), and a hard rubber or plastic ball. You can substitute the ball with a badminton bird. Mark off a "court" in the sand, yard, sidewalk, or driveway, with a dividing line down the center. The object of the game is to hit the ball back and forth over the line without letting it hit the ground or go out of bounds.

- ❑ Make your own miniature rain forest using an aquarium, fishbowl, or wide-mouthed glass jar.

  Cover the bottom with small stones, sand or charcoal to absorb the water; then add a thick layer of potting soil or dirt. Gently poke in small plants, ferns, and mosses.

  Water your plants only when necessary. You may leave the top open or cover it with a piece of plastic wrap or glass, removing the cover every so often if too much moisture accumulates. Pinching back the plants when they have grown too tall will make them fuller and more beautiful.

❑ Make Brigadeiro.

2 tablespoons margarine	1 can sweetened condensed milk
2 tablespoons cocoa	chocolate sprinkles

Directions: Mix the margarine, milk, and cocoa together. Cook over low heat, stirring continuously until thick. Remove from heat and cool completely. Grease your hands with margarine and roll the chocolate into small balls. Roll the ball in chocolate sprinkles.

❑ Make a Brazilian meal from *Eat Your Way Around the World.*

Holidays and Celebrations

❑ http://en.wikipedia.org/wiki/Public_holidays_in_Brazil

❑ www.advancingwomen.com/holiday/holiday_brazil.html

Travel and Tourism

www.embratur.gov.br

Flag of Brazil

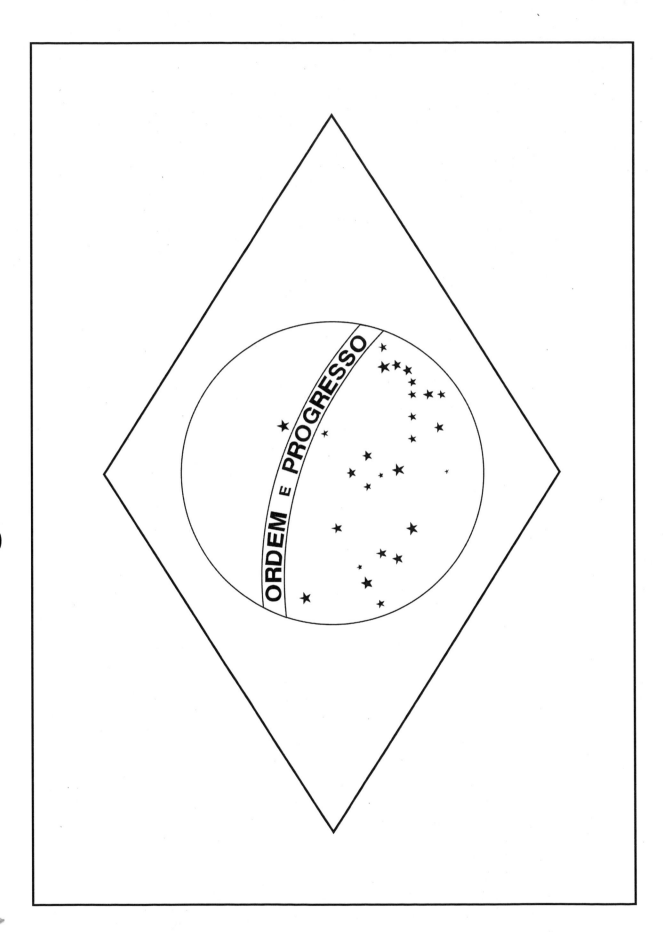

ORDEM E PROGRESSO

Brazil

Brazil

Venezuela

182

Population _____

Capital City _____

Religion _____

Type of Government _____

Currency _____

Language _____

What are the people called? _____

Venezuela

Venezuela

Situated on the northern edge of the Andes Mountains, Venezuela is a leading producer of petroleum. Before the discovery of oil in the 1920s, Venezuela was a poor agricultural country that depended heavily on its production of cacao, coffee, and sugarcane. The capital city is Caracas.

The flag of Venezuela is a yellow, blue, and red horizontal tricolor with a semi-circle of seven white stars in the center. Blue shows Venezuela's independence from Spain. The stars symbolize the seven provinces that supported that independence. Red stands for courage.

When 16th century explorers landed in what is now Venezuela, the houses on poles over the water reminded them of Venice, Italy. As a result, they called the area Venezuela which is Spanish for "Little Venice." The Spanish controlled the region until 1811 when Venezuela declared its independence.

Geography
- ❑ Highland
  - *Geography from A to Z,* page 23

History and Biographies
- ❑ Simón Bolívar
  - *A Picture Book of Simón Bolívar* – David A. Adler
  - *Simón Bolívar: Latin American Liberator* – Frank De Varona

General References
- ❑ *Venezuela* (A True Book) – Ann Heinrichs
- ❑ *Take a trip to Venezuela* – Keith Lye
- ❑ *Venezuela* – Patrick Merrick

Language Arts
- ❑ Choose from the Language Arts Suggestions on page 6.

Science
- ❑ Anteater
  - *Zoo Guide,* page 41
  - *Magnificent Mammals,* page 26
  - *Anteaters, Sloths, and Armadillos* – Ann O. Squire
  - www.enchantedlearning.com/subjects/mammals/anteater/Anteaterprintout.shtml
  - http://animals.nationalgeographic.com/animals/mammals/giant-anteater.html

- ❑ Giant Armadillo
  - *Pocket Factfiles: Mammals*, pages 220–221
  - *Anteaters, Sloths, and Armadillos* – Ann O. Squire
  - www.enchantedlearning.com/subjects/mammals/armadillo/9bandedprintout.shtml
  - http://animals.nationalgeographic.com/animals/mammals/armadillo.html
- ❑ Jaguar
  - *Pocket Factfiles: Mammals*, pages 18–19
  - www.enchantedlearning.com/subjects/mammals/cats/jaguar/Jaguarprintout.shtml
  - http://animals.nationalgeographic.com/animals/mammals/jaguar.html

Activities

- ❑ Color the flag of Venezuela.
- ❑ Color or label a map of Venezuela.
- ❑ Label the Caribbean Sea on a world map.
- ❑ Do a ceramics project.
- ❑ Make Quesillo.

¼ cup sugar	⅛ cup water
4 eggs	1 can evaporated milk
1 can sweetened condensed milk	1 teaspoon vanilla

Directions: In an ovenproof pan, boil the sugar and water, tilting the pan to coat. Do not brown. Mix the remaining ingredients in a blender. Pour the mixture into the caramelled pan. Refrigerate, then bake for 1 hour at 350°F or until a knife inserted into the Quesillo comes out clean.

- ❑ Make a Venezuelan meal from *Eat Your Way Around the World.*

Holidays and Celebrations

- ❑ http://en.wikipedia.org/wiki/Holidays_in_Venezuela
- ❑ www.californiamall.com/holidaytraditions/traditions-Venezuela.htm

Travel and Tourism

Venezuelan Tourism Association
Box 3010
Sausalito, CA 94966

Telephone: 415-331-0100

Email: vtajb@hotmail.com

Website: www.think-venezuela.net

Flag of Venezuela

Venezuela

185

Peru

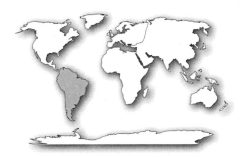

186

Population _____

Capital City _____

Religion _____

Type of Government _____

Currency _____

Language _____

What are the people called? _____

Peru

Peru

Located on the west coast of South America, Peru is a land of extreme contrast. On the west side of Peru is desert that is drier than the Sahara, and on the east side are rain forests and jungles that receive over 80 inches of rain a year. The center of the country is dominated by the Andes Mountains. High in the Andes Mountains, on Peru's border with Bolivia, is Lake Titicaca, the largest lake in South America and the world's highest lake that man can navigate. Lima is the capital city.

The flag of Peru is red, white, and red vertical bands with the country's coat of arms in the center. The cornucopia on the coat of arms is said to represent prosperity.

The prosperity symbolized on the coat of arms is something most Peruvians never experience. Even though their homeland is a leading producer of silver, copper, lead, and zinc, the majority of Peruvians are poor. Most of them work in low paying jobs in the cities or as small farmers growing little more than enough to feed their families.

Geography
❑ Mountain Pass
- *Geography from A to Z,* page 31

History and Biographies
❑ Francisco Pizarro
- *Francisco Pizarro and the Conquest of the Inca* – Gina DeAngelis
- www.enchantedlearning.com/explorers/page/p/pizarro.shtml

General References
❑ *A Family in Peru* – Jetty St. John
❑ *Take a Trip to Peru* – Keith Lye
❑ *My Amazon River Day* – Kris Nesbitt
❑ *Tomasino: A Child of Peru* – Hervé Giraud
❑ *Peru* – Kristin Thoennes
❑ *Peru* – Marycate O'Sullivan

Literature
❑ *Missionary Stories with the Millers,* chapter 14
❑ *Miro in the Kingdom of the Sun* – Jane Kurtz

Language Arts

❑ Choose from the Language Arts Suggestions on page 6.

❑ Keep a journal in a bound book as if you were a member of Francisco Pizarro's exploration party encountering the Incas. Refer to the *Big Book of Books and Activities*, page 50.

Science

❑ Sloth
  - *Zoo Guide*, page 87
  - *Pocket Factfiles: Mammals,* pages 218–219
  - *Magnificent Mammals,* page 60
  - *Tropical Forest Animals* – Elaine Landau
  - *Anteaters, Sloths, and Armadillos* – Ann O. Squire
  - www.enchantedlearning.com/subjects/mammals/sloth/
  - www.zooatlanta.org/home/animals/mammals/sloth
  - http://kids.nationalgeographic.com/Animals/CreatureFeature/Sloths

Activities

❑ Color or make the flag of Peru.

❑ Color or label a map of Peru.

❑ Label the Andes Mountains on a world map.

❑ Make Peruvian Caramel Sauce with Fruit.

12 oz. evaporated milk	2 cups milk
½ teaspoon baking soda	1½ cups packed brown sugar
¼ cup water	fruit

Directions: Heat evaporated milk, milk, and baking soda to boiling; remove from heat. Heat brown sugar and water in Dutch oven over low heat, stirring constantly, until sugar is dissolved. Add milk mixture. Cook uncovered over medium-low heat, stirring frequently, until mixture is very thick and golden brown, about 1 hour. Pour into serving bowl. Cover and refrigerate at least 4 hours. Serve with fruit.

❑ Make a Peruvian meal from *Eat Your Way Around the World*.

Bible

❑ *Missionary Stories with the Millers*, chapter 14
  - I Thessalonians 5:18

Holidays and Celebrations

❑ http://en.wikipedia.org/wiki/List_of_public_holidays_in_Peru

❑ www.cuscoperu.com/cusco/qosqo/1t7_fiestas.htm

Travel and Tourism

www.peru.info/default.asp?leng=2

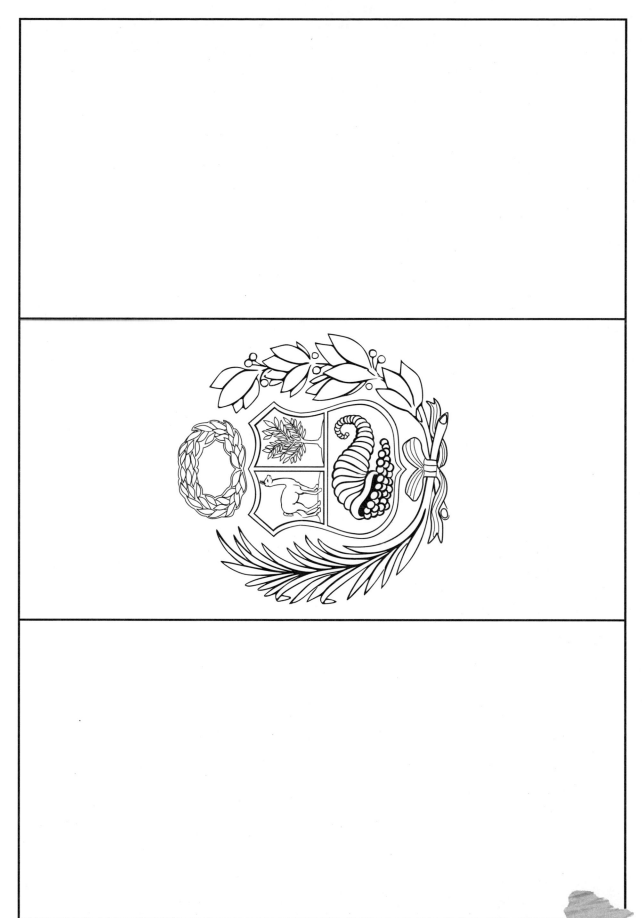

Flag of Peru

Peru

Argentina

Population _____

Capital City _____

Religion _____

Type of Government _____

Currency _____

Language _____

What are the people called? _____

Argentina

Argentina

A long, tapering country that occupies most of the southern part of the continent, Argentina is the second largest country in South America. Divided into four geographical regions: the Andes, the Pampas, the Patagonia, and the northern plain, the landscape of Argentina varies dramatically. The capital city is Buenos Aires.

The flag of Argentina is three horizontal bands of sky blue, white, and sky blue with the Sun of May in the center. The flag did not have the sun on it when it was adopted in 1812. It was added in 1818.

Argentina received its name from Spanish settlers in search of their fortune. They took the name from *argentum* which is Latin for "silver."

Geography
- ❑ Pampas
  - *Geography from A to Z,* page 21

General References
- ❑ *Argentina* – Michael Burgan
- ❑ *Children Just Like Me,* pages 12–13
- ❑ *Argentina* – Muriel L. Dubois
- ❑ *Argentina* – Kathryn Stevens

Literature
- ❑ *On the Pampas* – Maria Cristina Brusca
- ❑ *My Mama's Little Ranch on the Pampas* – Maria Cristina Brusca

Language Arts
- ❑ Choose from the Language Arts Suggestions on page 6.

Science
- ❑ Squid
  - *Aquarium Guide,* page 167
  - http://en.wikipedia.org/wiki/Squid
- ❑ Rhea
  - http://en.wikipedia.org/wiki/Rhea_(bird)

Activities

- ❑ Color the flag of Argentina.
- ❑ Color or label a map of Argentina.
- ❑ Shade the Pampas on a world map.
- ❑ Play rayuela (hopscotch).
- ❑ Make Dulce de Leche (Sweet Milk Dessert).

    2 cans sweetened condensed milk   ice cream or butter cookies

    Directions: Shake cans of milk. Place unopened cans in a saucepan and cover completely with water. Boil the cans for an hour and a half, making sure the cans are always covered with water. Do not open cans until they are completely cool. Pour the butterscotch-type sauce over ice cream or spread between two butter cookies.

- ❑ Make an Argentine meal from *Eat Your Way Around the World.*

Bible

- ❑ *On the Pampas*
    - Proverbs 12:10
    - Matthew 7:11

Holidays and Celebrations

- ❑ http://en.wikipedia.org/wiki/Public_holidays_in_Argentina/
- ❑ www.geographia.com/argentina/calendar.htm

Travel and Tourism

Argentina Government Tourist Office
12 West 56th Street
New York, NY 10019

Telephone: 212-603-0443

www.turismo.gov.ar

Flag of Argentina

Argentina

South America Review Map

See how many countries you can identify. Write their names on the map.

© 2003 Geography Matters   ad majorem Dei gloriam!

194

195

Africa

Africa is the second largest continent and has the second largest population. Africa boasts the world's largest desert, the Sahara, and the world's longest river, the Nile. Africa is a land of rain forests, grassy plains, and deserts. The highest point in Africa is at Kilamanjaro, Tasmania (19,340 ft) and its lowest point is Lac Assal, Dijbouti (515 ft. below sea level). Africa is bordered by the Indian Ocean on the east and the Atlantic Ocean on the west.

Africa

Color each country you study.

Tunisia
Morocco
Algeria
Libya
Egypt
Western Sahara
Mauritania
Mali
Niger
Chad
Sudan
Eritrea
Gambia
Senegal
Burkina Faso
Djibouti
Guinea-Bissau
Guinea
Nigeria
Ethiopia
Sierra Leone
Cote d'Ivoire
Ghana
Central African Republic
Somalia
Liberia
Togo
Benin
Cameroon
Equatorial Guinea
Uganda
Kenya
Gabon
Congo
Democratic Republic of the Congo
Rwanda
Burundi
Tanzania
Angola
Malawi
Zambia
Mozambique
Namibia
Zimbabwe
Madagascar
Botswana
Swaziland
South Africa
Lesotho

© 2003 Geography Matters

ad majorem Dei gloriam!

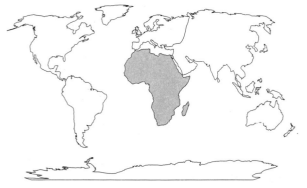

Africa

198

Africa

Africa

Africa is the second-largest continent, covering about twenty percent of the world's land area. Most of Africa is a plateau, surrounded by narrow coastal plains. Kilimanjaro, an inactive volcano in Tanzania, is the highest peak. The Nile, Congo, and Niger are the major rivers. The continent has two main people groups. North of the Sahara are the Arabs and Berbers who speak Arabic and practice Islam. South of the Sahara are the black Africans that are divided into over one thousand ethnic groups. Africa contains many of the world's poorest countries.

General References

- ❑ *The Asante of West Africa* – Jamie Hetfield
- ❑ *Our Father's World,* pages 85–92
- ❑ *African Adventures* – Dick Anderson (available from Timberdoodle)
- ❑ *Africa* – Mike Graf
- ❑ *Good Morning, Africa!* – April Pulley Sayre

Literature

- ❑ *Africa Calling* – Daniel Alderman
- ❑ *Ashanti to Zulu* – Margaret Musgrove
- ❑ *Uncommon Traveler: Mary Kingsley in Africa* – Don Brown
- ❑ *Where Are You Going, Manyoni?* – Catherine Stock
- ❑ *Zzng! Zzng! Zzng!* – Phyllis Gershator
- ❑ *A Country Far Away* – Nigel Gray
- ❑ *Koi and the Kola Nuts* – Verna Aardema
- ❑ *Off to the Sweet Shores of Africa* – Uzo Unobagha
- ❑ *Missionary Stories with the Millers,* chapters 1, 4, 7
- ❑ *Great for God (Heaven's Heroes),* chapters 1, 7, 11
- ❑ *The Night Has Ears* – Ashley Bryan

Language Arts

- ❑ Choose from the Language Arts Suggestions on page 6.
- ❑ Use the proverbs in *The Night Has Ears* as copy work.

Science

- ❑ *African Animals* – Caroline Arnold
- ❑ *Jungle Jack Hanna's Safari Adventure* – Jack Hanna and Rick A. Prebeg
- ❑ *On Safari* – Tessa Paul
- ❑ http://video.nationalgeographic.com/video/wildcamafrica/ – Provides real time video of animal habitats in Africa
- ❑ Ape and Monkey
  - *Monkeys and Apes* (A New True Book) – Kathryn Wentzel Lumley
  - *Chimpanzees* (A True Book) – Patricia A. Fink Martin
  - *Gorillas* (A True Book) – Patricia A. Fink Martin
  - *Gorillas: Gentle Giants of the Forest* – Joyce Milton
  - *Pocket Factfiles: Mammals,* pages 120–121
  - *Magnificent Mammals,* page 32
  - www.enchantedlearning.com/themes/monkeys.shtml
  - www.crayola.com/free-coloring-pages/print/monkey-connect-the-dots-coloring-page/
  - http://animals.nationalgeographic.com/animals/photos/monkeys.html

Bible

- ❑ *Missionary Stories with the Millers,* chapter 1
  - Psalm 91
- ❑ *Missionary Stories with the Millers,* chapter 4
  - Exodus 15:26b
  - Matthew 4:23b
- ❑ *Missionary Stories with the Millers,* chapter 7
  - Nehemiah 8:10
  - Matthew 9:27–31
- ❑ Ape
  - 2 Chronicles 9:21

Holidays and Celebrations

- ❑ www.inithebabeandsuckling.com/africaday.html
- ❑ www.santas.net/africanchristmas.htm

FIND THE TWINS

Which two are exactly alike?

3

6

2

5

1

4

201

Africa

MAZE CRAZE

Africa

Crossword Puzzle

Across
3 I am like a monkey, but I do not have a tail.
4 I am the largest member of the ape family.
6 I am like an ape, but I have a tail.
9 I am a member of the ape family.
10 I am the second largest land mammal. Only the elephant is bigger.

Down
1 I have black and white stripes.
2 I have a long neck.
5 I have a thick mane.
7 I am a bird that cannot fly.
8 I have a big horn coming out of my forehead.

Africa

Word Search

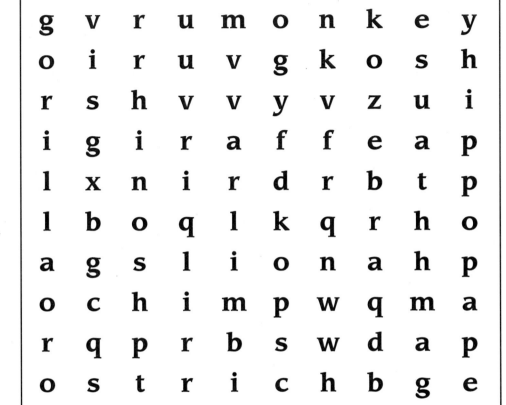

g	v	r	u	m	o	n	k	e	y
o	i	r	u	v	g	k	o	s	h
r	s	h	v	v	y	v	z	u	i
i	g	i	r	a	f	f	e	a	p
l	x	n	i	r	d	r	b	t	p
l	b	o	q	l	k	q	r	h	o
a	g	s	l	i	o	n	a	h	p
o	c	h	i	m	p	w	q	m	a
r	q	p	r	b	s	w	d	a	p
o	s	t	r	i	c	h	b	g	e

ape
chimp
giraffe
gorilla
hippo

lion
monkey
ostrich
rhino
zebra

Africa

205

Africa

South Africa

Population _____

Capital City _____

Religion _____

Type of Government _____

Currency _____

Language _____

What are the people called? _____

206

South Africa

On the southern tip of Africa, between the Indian Ocean and the Atlantic Ocean, lies South Africa. It has the largest European, Indian, and mixed race populations on the continent, making it the most ethnically diverse country in Africa. South Africa has three capitals – Cape Town (legislative), Pretoria (administrative), and Bloemfontein (judicial).

The colorful flag of South Africa was adopted in 1994. Yellow, black, and green were taken from the flag of the African National Congress and represent the people, land, and riches. The red, white, and blue were the colors of the Boer Republics. The Y-shaped design signifies unification and a merging of tradition and progress.

Racial problems have played a major role in South Africa's history and politics. Apartheid was a policy of racial segregation and discrimination that determined where a person could live, how much education they could receive, and what kind of work they could do based on the color of their skin. A formal end to apartheid was declared in 1990.

Geography
❑ Cape
- *Geography from A to Z*, page 11

History and Biographies
❑ Nelson Mandela
- www.biography.com/blackhistory/featured-biography/nelson-mandela.jsp

❑ Zulu
- *The Zulu Kingdom* – Sandra Klopper
- *A Zulu Family* – Nancy Durrell McKenna
- *The Zulu of Southern Africa* – Christine Cornell

General References
❑ *South Africa* (A New True Book) – Karen Jacobsen
❑ *South Africa* – Ann Heinrichs
❑ *Letters from Around the World: South Africa* – Cath Senker
❑ *South Africa* – Lucia Raatma

Literature
❑ *Missionary Stories with the Millers*, chapter 24
❑ *Jaffa's Journey* – Hugh Lewin
❑ *Jaffa's Mother* – Hugh Lewin

- ❑ *Jaffa's Father* – Hugh Lewin
- ❑ *Magical Tales from Many Lands* – Margaret Mayo, "Uranana and the Enormous One Tusked Elephant"
- ❑ *Magnificent Mammals,* page 22

Language Arts

- ❑ Choose from the Language Arts Suggestions on page 6.
- ❑ If you read the Jaffa books listed above, let the student make up an additional story such as "Jaffa's Brother" or "Jaffa's Friend."

Science

- ❑ Boer Goats
  - • http://www.zooatlanta.org/home/animals/mammals/boer_goat
- ❑ Meerkat
  - • *Zoo Guide,* page 63
  - • www.zooatlanta.org/home/animals/mammals/meerkat
  - • http://kids.nationalgeographic.com/Animals/CreatureFeature/Meerkat
- ❑ Cheetah
  - • *Zoo Guide,* page 163
  - • *Cheetahs* – Ann O. Squire
  - • *Magnificent Mammals,* page 18
  - • http://kids.nationalgeographic.com/Animals/CreatureFeature/Cheetah
- ❑ www.wildcam.com/public/index.jsp

Activities

- ❑ Color the flag of South Africa.
- ❑ Color or label a map of South Africa.
- ❑ Label the Cape of Good Hope on a world map.
- ❑ Make a South African meal from *Eat Your Way Around the World.*

Bible

- ❑ *Missionary Stories with the Millers,* chapter 24
  - • 2 Corinthians 5:17

Holidays and Celebrations

- ❑ http://en.wikipedia.org/wiki/Public_holidays_in_South_Africa?
- ❑ www.places.co.za/html/traveli_social.html#publicholiday

Travel and Tourism

South African Tourism
500 Fifth Avenue, Ste 2040
New York, NY 10110

Telephone: 1-800-822-5368 (toll free in USA)
Telephone: 212-730-2929

Email: satourny@aol.com
Website: www.southafrica.net
www.environment.gov.za

Flag of South Africa

South Africa

209

Kenya

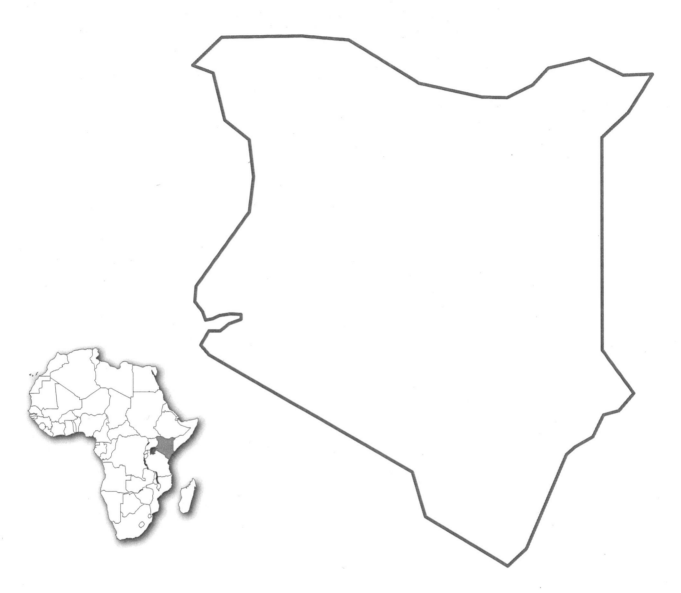

Population _____

Capital City _____

Religion _____

Type of Government _____

Currency _____

Language _____

What are the people called? _____

Kenya

Kenya

Kenya is an east African country known for its variety of wildlife. People from all over the world come to Kenya to go on safari to see animals such as elephants, giraffes, lions, and cheetahs. The capital of Kenya is Nairobi.

The flag of Kenya is three equal bands of black, red, and green with smaller white bands on either side of the red. Black, red, and green are the colors of the KANU political party and symbolize the people, their struggle for independence, and agriculture. The shield in the center of the flag represents defense and freedom.

The Great Rift Valley is a large, deep depression that runs from southwest Asia to southeast Africa. In Kenya, the Great Rift Valley is 50 miles wide, 375 miles long, 2,000 feet deep, and runs north and south through the western portion of the country. The Valley has some of the most fertile soil in Africa, making it an important farming area.

Geography
- ❑ Lake
  - *Geography from A to Z,* page 27
- ❑ Valley
  - *Geography from A to Z,* page 43

History and Biographies
- ❑ Maasai
  - *The Maasai of East Africa* – Jamie Hetfield
- ❑ Verna Aardema (Verna Aardema is not from Kenya, but so many of her books are listed in this section that this would be a good time to learn about her.)
  - *A Bookworm Who Hatched* – Verna Aardema

General References
- ❑ *Next Stop Kenya* – Fred Martin
- ❑ *A Family in Kenya* – Lerner Publications Company
- ❑ *Kenya* – Lucia Raatma (Reference to millions of years.)
- ❑ *Letters from Around the World: Kenya* – Ali Brownlie
- ❑ *Kenya ABCs* – Sarah Heiman
- ❑ *Kenya* – Michael Dahl (Makes a reference to early humans.)

Literature

- ☐ *Moja Means One: Swahili Counting Book* – Muriel Feelings
- ☐ *Rabbit Makes a Monkey of Lion* – Verna Aardema
- ☐ *The Lonely Lioness and the Ostrich Chicks* – Verna Aardema
- ☐ *Bringing the Rain to Kapiti Plain* – Verna Aardema
- ☐ *Who's in Rabbit's House* – Verna Aardema
- ☐ *How the Ostrich Got Its Long Neck* – Verna Aardema

Language Arts

- ☐ Choose from the Language Arts Suggestions on page 6.
- ☐ Have the child write and illustrate a story about going on a safari in Kenya.

Science

- ☐ Bongo
  - www.zooatlanta.org/home/animals/mammals/bongo
- ☐ Giraffe
  - *Zoo Guide*, page 45
  - *The Giraffe: A Living Tower* – Christine and Michel Denis-Huot
  - *Pocket Factfiles: Mammals*, pages 150–151
  - *Magnificent Mammals*, page 30
  - *Giraffe* – Caroline Arnold
  - www.enchantedlearning.com/themes/giraffe.shtml
  - www.zooatlanta.org/home/animals/mammals/giraffe
  - http://animals.nationalgeographic.com/animals/mammals/giraffe.html
  - http://kids.nationalgeographic.com/Animals/CreatureFeature/Giraffe
- ☐ Hippopotamus
  - *Zoo Guide*, page 51
  - *Pocket Factfiles: Mammals*, pages 138–139
  - *Magnificent Mammals*, page 36
  - *Hippos* – Sally M. Walker
  - *Hippos* – Miriam Schlein (Note: You may want to skip the first two chapters due to evolutionary content.)
  - *Hippo* – Caroline Arnold
  - www.familycorner.com/family/kids/color/hippo.shtml
  - http://animals.nationalgeographic.com/animals/mammals/hippopotamus.html
  - http://kids.nationalgeographic.com/Animals/CreatureFeature/Hippopotamus
- ☐ Lion
  - *Zoo Guide*, page 171
  - *Pocket Factfiles: Mammals*, pages 10–11
  - *Magnificent Mammals*, page 40
  - *Lions* – Cynthia Overbeck
  - *Lion* – Caroline Arnold
  - http://coloring-page.net/activity/pages/dot-1.html
  - www.zooatlanta.org/home/animals/mammals/african_lion
  - http://animals.nationalgeographic.com/animals/mammals/african-lion.html
  - http://kids.nationalgeographic.com/Animals/CreatureFeature/Lion

- ❑ Ostrich
    - *Zoo Guide,* page 141
    - *Ostriches* (A New True Book) – Emilie U. Lepthien
    - www.enchantedlearning.com/subjects/birds/printouts/Ostrichcoloring.shtml
    - http://animals.nationalgeographic.com/animals/birds/ostrich.html
    - http://kids.nationalgeographic.com/Animals/CreatureFeature/Ostrich
- ❑ Schmidts Guenons
    - www.zooatlanta.org/home/animals/mammals/schmidts_guenons
- ❑ Zebra
    - *Zoo Guide,* page 109
    - *Pocket Factfiles: Mammals,* pages 130–131
    - *Magnificent Mammals,* page 68
    - *Zebra* – Caroline Arnold
    - www.enchantedlearning.com/subjects/mammals/zebra/Zebracoloring.shtml
    - www.zooatlanta.org/home/animals/mammals/zebra
    - http://animals.nationalgeographic.com/animals/mammals/zebra.html
    - http://kids.nationalgeographic.com/Animals/CreatureFeature/Zebra

Activities

- ❑ Color the flag of Kenya.
- ❑ Color or label the map of Kenya.
- ❑ Label the equator and Lake Victoria on a world map. Shade in the Great Rift Valley.
- ❑ Make Irio.

    ¼lb corn　　　　　3lb potatoes, mashed　　　　　½lb peas

    Directions: Bring corn and peas to a boil. Reduce heat and simmer until done. Drain. Mix with mashed potatoes. Add salt to taste.

- ❑ Make a Kenyan meal from *Eat Your Way Around the World.*

Bible

- ❑ Lion
    - Psalm 17:12
    - Proverbs 28:1
    - Proverbs 30:30
    - Daniel 6
    - Amos 3:4
    - Nahum 2:11–12
- ❑ Ostrich
    - Job 39:13–18
    - Lamentations 4:3

Holidays and Celebrations

- ❑ *Festivals of the World: Kenya* – Falaq Kagda
- ❑ www.cp-pc.ca/english/kenya/holidays.html

Travel and Tourism

Embassy of the Republic of Kenya
22249 R Street N.W.
Washington, D.C.20008

Telephone: 202-387-6101
Email: info@kenyaembassy.com
Website: www.kenyaembassy.com

Flag of Kenya

214

Kenya

Kenya

Morocco

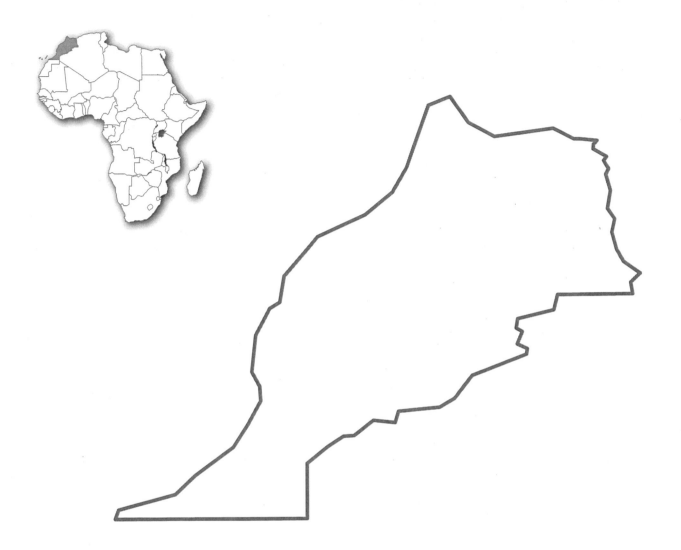

Population _____

Capital City _____

Religion _____

Type of Government _____

Currency _____

Language _____

What are the people called? _____

216

Morocco

Separated from Europe by a narrow stretch of the Strait of Gibraltar, Morocco is a small country in northern Africa. The Atlas Mountains cover most of the country and have some of the highest peaks in North Africa. Rabat is the capital of Morocco.

The flag of Morocco includes a green pentacle, or five-pointed star called the Seal of Solomon, centered on a red field. The pentacle symbolizes the link between God and the nation.

Morocco and the United States have a long standing friendship. In 1777, Morocco became the first country to recognize the newly formed United States of America. In 1783, the Moroccan-American Treaty of Friendship was signed. It is the United States' oldest non-broken friendship treaty. The land purchased for the United States consulate in Tangier, Morocco, was the first property that the United States owned abroad.

Geography
❑ Strait
- *Geography from A to Z,* page 41

General References
❑ *A Family in Morocco* – Judy Stewart

❑ *Morocco* – Bob Italia

❑ *Take a Trip to Morocco* – Keith Lye

❑ *The Children of Morocco* – Jules Hermes

❑ *Children Just Like Me,* pages 40–41

❑ *Morocco* – Patrick Merrick

Literature
❑ *Ali, Child of the Desert* – Jonathan London

Language Arts
❑ Choose from the Language Arts Suggestions on page 6.

❑ Make a large matchbook describing the dress of Morocco. Refer to the *Big Book of Books and Activities,* page 26.

Activities
❑ Color the flag of Morocco.

❑ Color or make a map of Morocco.

❑ Label the Strait of Gibraltar on a world map.

❑ Make a Moroccan meal from *Eat Your Way Around the World.*

❑ Make Couscous with Chicken.

2 tablespoons olive oil	3 lb chicken, cut up
4 small carrots, sliced	2 medium onions, sliced
2 medium turnips, quartered	2 cloves garlic, minced
2 teaspoons ground coriander	1½ teaspoons salt
1 teaspoon chicken bouillon	¼ teaspoon red pepper
¼ teaspoon ground turmeric	1 cup water
3 zucchini, sliced	15 oz. can garbanzo beans
Couscous (recipe below)	

Directions: Heat oil in Dutch oven until hot. Cook chicken in oil until brown on all sides, about 15 minutes. Drain fat from Dutch oven. Add carrots, onions, turnips, garlic, coriander, salt, bouillon, ground red pepper, and turmeric. Pour water over vegetables. Heat to boiling; reduce heat. Cover and simmer 30 minutes.

Add zucchini to chicken mixture. Cover and cook until chicken is done, about 10 minutes.

Add beans; cook 5 minutes.

Prepare couscous. Mound in center of heated platter; arrange chicken and vegetables around couscous.

1⅓ cups couscous	¾ cup raisins
½ teaspoon salt	1 cup boiling water
½ cup butter	½ teaspoon ground turmeric

Mix couscous, raisins, and salt in 2-quart bowl; stir in boiling water. Let stand until all water is absorbed, 2 to 3 minutes. Heat butter in skillet until melted; stir in couscous and turmeric. Cook and stir 4 minutes.

Holidays and Celebrations

❑ www.morocco.com/discover/public-holidays/

❑ www.morocco.com/culture/celebrations/

Travel and Tourism

www.tourism-in-morocco.com/english/

Flag of Morocco

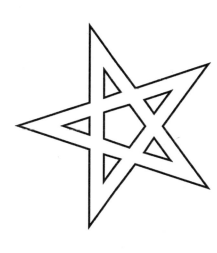

Nigeria

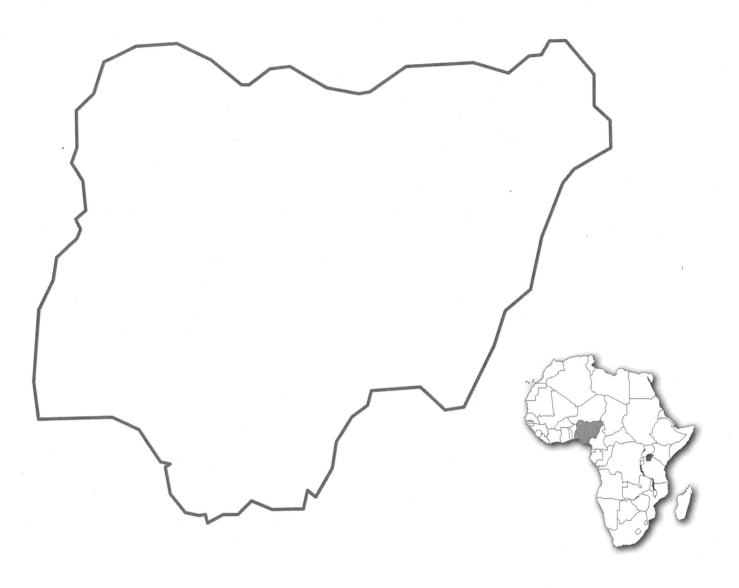

Population _____

Capital City _____

Religion _____

Type of Government _____

Currency _____

Language _____

What are the people called? _____

220

Nigeria

Nigeria

Nigeria is the most populated country in Africa. It is the size of Texas and New Mexico combined. Abuja became the capital of Nigeria in 1991.

Adopted in 1960 when the nation gained its independence from Great Britain, the flag of Nigeria is a green, white, and green tricolor. Green symbolizes the land and agriculture. White stands for peace and unity.

Hundreds of years ago, Nigeria developed from a number of kingdoms. Today, Nigeria has over two hundred fifty ethnic groups giving the country a rich culture and many challenges.

History and Biographies

❑ Mary Slessor
- *Ten Girls Who Changed the World* – Irene Howat, pages 67–80
- www.wholesomewords.org/biography/biorpslessor.html

❑ King Eyo Honesty VII

❑ Yoruba
- *The Yoruba of West Africa* – Jamie Hetfield
- http://en.wikipedia.org/wiki/Yoruba_people

General References

❑ *A Family in Nigeria* – Carol Barker

❑ *Take a Trip to Nigeria* – Keith Lye

❑ *Saying Good-bye* – Ifeoma Onyefulu

❑ *Nigeria: the People* – Bobbie Kalman

❑ *Nigeria* – Kristin Thoemes

Literature

❑ A Nigerian fable:

The chief sent out messengers to announce that he would give a feast and asked each guest to bring one calabash of palm wine. One man wanted very much to attend, but he had no wine to bring. When his wife suggested that he buy the wine, he said, "What! Spend money so that I can attend a feast that is free?" He thought to himself, "If hundreds of people were to pour their wine into the chief's pot, could just one calabash of water spoil so much wine?

The day of the feast came. Everyone bathed and dressed in their best clothes and gathered at the house of the chief. There was music and festive dancing. Each man, as he entered the chief's compound, poured the contents of his calabash into a large earthen pot. The man poured his water into the pot and greeted the chief.

221

When all the guests had arrived, the chief ordered his servants to fill everyone's cup with wine. The man was impatient, for there was nothing so refreshing as palm wine. At the chief's signal, all the guests put the cups to their lips and tasted...and tasted again...for what they tasted was not palm wine, but water. Each guest had thought that his one calabash of water could not spoil a great pot of palm wine.

❑ *Beat the Story Drum, Pum-Pum* – Ashley Bryan

❑ *Why Mosquitoes Buzz in People's Ears* – Verna Aardema

❑ *Mogo, the Third Warthog* – Donna Jo Napoli

Language Arts

❑ Choose from the Language Arts Suggestions on page 6.

❑ Describe the naming ceremony in Nigeria and have the child research the meaning of his/her own name. Have them include the reason their parents chose their particular name.

Science

❑ Warthog

- *Zoo Guide,* page 99
- www.zooatlanta.org/home/animals/mammals/warthog
- http://kids.nationalgeographic.com/Animals/CreatureFeature/Warthog

❑ Waterbuck

- www.zooatlanta.org/home/animals/mammals/waterbuck

Activities

❑ Color or make the flag of Nigeria.

❑ Color or label the map of Nigeria.

❑ Label the Niger River on a world map.

❑ Play Mancala (popular in Nigeria).

❑ Make Banana Fritters.

2½ cup flour	½ cup sugar
2 teaspoons cinnamon	2 eggs
1 cup milk	6 bananas, mashed
oil	confectioner's sugar

Directions: Combine flour, sugar, and cinnamon. Beat in eggs. Gradually add milk and beat until smooth. Stir in bananas. Pour batter by ¼ cupfuls onto hot griddle. Cook 2–3 minutes each side. Sprinkle with confectioner's sugar before serving.

❑ Make a Nigerian drum.

Small clay flowerpot	markers or paint
Paper grocery bag	paper taper

Decorate outside of flowerpot with markers or paint. Let dry. Cut a circle from the paper bag 3″ bigger than the open end of the flowerpot. Dampen circle and lay it over open end of flower pot. Pull the bag tight and tape it in place. Wrap the tape around several times. Allow to dry and enjoy the beautiful music.

❑ Make African beads.

4 cups flour	2 cups salt
2 cups water	large bowl
baking tray	toothpicks
acrylic paints	shellac
string	

Mix together flour and salt. Gradually add water and knead dough until thoroughly mixed and smooth. Form small beads out of the dough. Fifteen to twenty beads will be needed for each necklace. Push a toothpick through the center of each bead to make a hole. Bake 15–20 minutes in a 350° F oven. Cool completely. Decorate beads with paint and let dry. Shellac beads and allow to dry over night. Strings beads.

❑ Make a Nigerian meal from *Eat Your Way Around the World*.

Holidays and Celebrations

❑ www.motherlandnigeria.com/holidays.html

Travel and Tourism

www.euromonitor.com/Travel_And_Tourism_in_Nigeria

Flag of Nigeria

224

Nigeria

Nigeria

Egypt

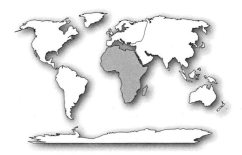

226

Population _____

Capital City _____

Religion _____

Type of Government _____

Currency _____

Language _____

What are the people called? _____

Egypt

Egypt

Famous for its ancient pyramids, Egypt is a dry desert country that lies mostly in northeastern Africa. A small part of the country known as the Sinai Peninsula is actually a part of Asia. The capital of Egypt is Cairo, Africa's largest city.

Adopted in 1984, the flag of Egypt is a red, white, and black horizontal tricolor with the golden Eagle of Saladin in the center.

More than ninety percent of Egypt is uninhabited desert. Ninety-nine percent of the Egyptian people live near the country's few waterways. The Nile River, which flows north through Egypt and empties into the Mediterranean Sea, is the world's longest river.

Geography
- ❑ Nile River
- ❑ Delta
  - *Geography from A to Z,* page 15
  - *Usborne Internet-linked Science Encyclopedia,* page 191

History and Biographies
- ❑ Cleopatra
  - *Cleopatra* – Diane Stanley
- ❑ King Tutankhamen
  - *Tutankhamen* – Robert Green
  - *Tut's Mummy: Lost and Found* – Judy Donnelly
- ❑ Hatshepsut
  - *Hatshepsut: First Female Pharaoh* – Peggy Pancella

General References
- ❑ *A Family in Egypt* - Olivia Bennett
- ❑ *Take a Trip to Egypt* – Keith Lye
- ❑ *The Children of Egypt* – Matti A. Pitkanen
- ❑ *Children Just Like Me,* page 36

Literature
- ❑ *Bill and Pete Go Down the Nile* – Tomie dePaola
- ❑ *The Day of Ahmed's Secret* – Florence Parry Heide and Judith Heide Gilliland
- ❑ *Missionary Stories with the Millers,* chapters 2 and 9

Language Arts

❑ Choose from the Language Arts Suggestions on page 6.

❑ Make a layered book about the plagues of Egypt listed in Exodus 5–11. Refer to the *Big Book of Books and Activities*, page 70.

❑ Write an adventure story about taking a trip down the Nile. Encourage your child to use their imagination and describe encounters with various animals.

Science

❑ Deserts
  • *Geography A to Z,* page 17
  • *One Day in the Desert* – Jean Craighead George
  • *Deserts* – Elsa Posell
  • *Deserts* – Keith Brandt
  • *Welcome to the Sea of Sand* – Jane Yolen
  • *Desert* – April Pulley Sayre
  • *Earth Science for Every Kid* – Janice Van Cleave – experiment 49

Activities

❑ *Pyramids! 50 Hands-on Activities to Experience Ancient Egypt* – Avery Hart and Paul Mantell

❑ Color the flag of Egypt.

❑ Color or label the map of Egypt.

❑ Label the Nile River and Red Sea on a world map. Shade in the Sinai Peninsula and the Sahara Desert.

❑ Make the Rosetta Stone.

Roll soft clay into clean meat trays. The children can carve their own hieroglyphs with Popsicle sticks, toothpicks, or the end of a paintbrush. Follow manufacturers directions for drying clay.

❑ If you read *The Day of Ahmed's Secret* with a young child, have the child practice writing his name.

❑ Make an Egyptian meal from *Eat Your Way Around the World.*

❑ Go to www.mce.k12tn.net/ancient_egypt/directions.htm for a variety of Egyptian craft ideas.

❑ Go to www.crayola.com/free-coloring-pages/print/great-pyramids-coloring-page/ for a printable pyramid to cut and color.

❑ Make a chicken mummy. For instructions, go to www.mummytombs.com/mummymaking/mummychicken3.htm.

Bible

❑ The story of Joseph
  • Genesis 37
  • Genesis 39–47
  • Genesis 50:15–26

❑ The story of Moses
  • Exodus 2–4

❑ The plagues of Egypt
  • Exodus 5–11

- ❑ Passover – the Children of Israel protected
    - Exodus 12:1–30
- ❑ Children of Israel delivered from slavery.
    - Exodus 12:31–51
- ❑ Mary and Joseph flee to Egypt
    - Matthew 2:13–15
- ❑ *Missionary Stories with the Millers*, chapter 2
    - Exodus 20:15
    - Acts 16:30–31
- ❑ *Missionary Stories with the Millers*, chapter 9
    - Mark 10:13–17

Holidays and Celebrations

- ❑ www.cp-pc.ca/english/egypt/holidays.html
- ❑ www.santas.net/egyptianchristmas.htm

Travel and Tourism

Egyptian Tourist Authority
645 N. Michigan Avenue Suite 829
Chicago, IL 60611

Telephone: 312-280-4666

Email: egyptmdwst@aol.com

Website: www.egypttourism.org

Flag of Egypt

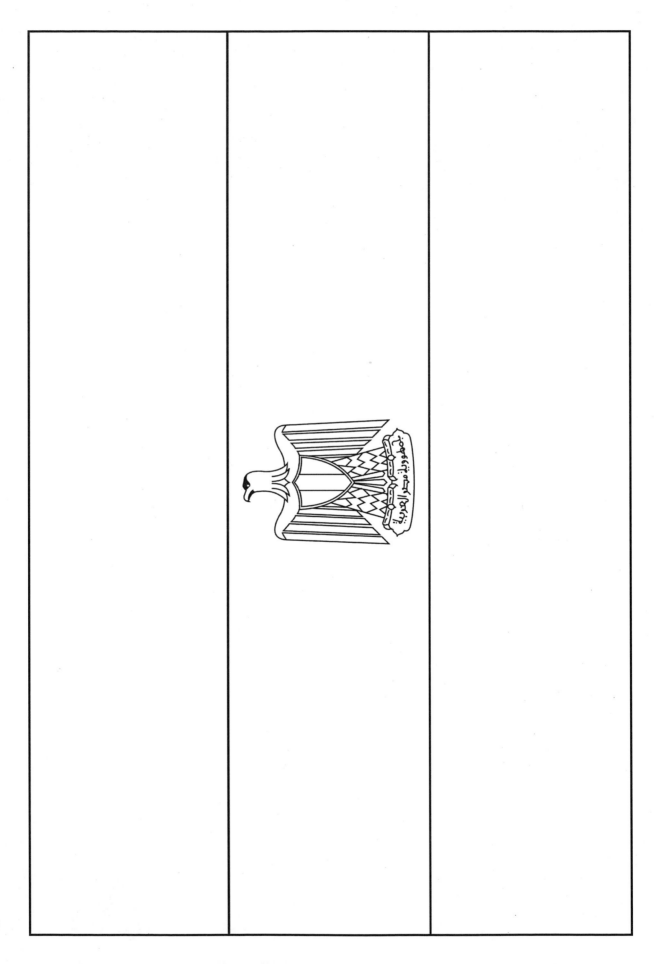

Egypt

Africa Review Map

See how many countries you can identify. Write their names on the map.

© 2003 Geography Matters

Oceania

Oceania includes the countries of Australia and New Zealand and the island groups known as Micronesia, Melanesia, and Polynesia. Oceania stretches from the Tropic of Cancer in the north to New Zealand in the south. The highest point in Oceania is Mt. Wilhelm in Papua New Guinea (14,793 ft.) and its lowest point is at Lake Eyre in South Australia where the elevation is measured 52 ft. below sea level. The continent of Australia is the largest land mass in Oceania.

Oceania

Color each country you study.

Papua
New Guinea

Australia

New
Zealand

© 2003 Geography Matters   ad majorem Dei gloriam!

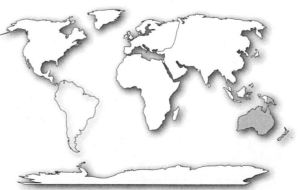

Australia

234

Population _____

Capital City _____

Religion _____

Type of Government _____

Currency _____

Language _____

What are the people called? _____

Australia

Australia

One of the world's driest landmasses, Australia is the only country that is also a continent. Because of its location south of the equator, Australia is commonly referred to as "the land down under." The capital city is Canberra.

The flag of Australia is the Union Jack of the United Kingdom in the right, upper corner, a large star representing the Commonwealth beneath it, and the Southern Cross constellation all on a field of blue. The Union Jack shows Australia's ties with Great Britain. Each point of the Commonwealth Star represents the federal states and territories. The Southern Cross is visible in the southern night sky year round.

The majority of Australia's wildlife can be found only in Australia. The kangaroo, koala, and duck-billed platypus are some of the more easily recognizable animals that are distinctly Australian.

Geography
❑ Reef
- *Geography from A to Z,* page 37

❑ Key
- *Geography from A to Z,* page 27

History and Biographies
❑ James Cook
- *Profiles from History,* page 113
- *A World Explorer: James Cook* – Adele deLeeuw
- *Captain Cook: Pacific Explorer* – Ronald Syrne
- www.enchantedlearning.com/explorers/page/c/cook.shtml

❑ Matthew Flinders
- www.enchantedlearning.com/explorers/page/f/flinders.shtml

❑ Robert Burke and William Wills
- www.enchantedlearning.com/explorers/page/b/burkewills.shtml

General References
❑ *Next Stop Australia* – Fred Martin

❑ *Passport to Australia* – Susan Pepper

❑ *A Family in Australia* – Emily Gunner and Shirley McConky

❑ *An Aboriginal Family* – Rollo Browne

❑ *Australia* – Mary Berendes

❑ *Children Just Like Me,* pages 76–77

❑ *Cooking the Australian Way* – Elizabeth Geramane

- ❑ *Australia* – Bob Italia
- ❑ *Australia* – Henry Pluckrose
- ❑ *Outback Adventures* – Jim Cromarty (available from Timberdoodle)
- ❑ *Australia ABCs* – Sarah Heiman
- ❑ *G'Day, Australia!* – April Pulley Sayre (mild evolution)
- ❑ *Australia* – Katie Bagley

Literature

- ❑ *The Pumpkin Runner* – Marsha Arnold
- ❑ *Koala Lou* – Mem Fox
- ❑ *Wombat Stew* – Marcia Vaughn
- ❑ *The Very Boastful Kangaroo* – Bernard Most
- ❑ *The Biggest Frog in Australia* – Susan L. Roth
- ❑ *The Singing Snake* – Stefan Czernecki
- ❑ *Magical Tales from Many Lands* – Margeret Mayo, "Koala"

Language Arts

- ❑ Choose from the Language Arts Suggestions on page 6.
- ❑ Write a poem or story about a koala and/or a kangaroo.
- ❑ Make a Circle Mobile describing one or more of the animals unique to Australia. Refer to the *Big Book of Books and Activities*, page 64.

Science

- ❑ *Top to Bottom Down Under* – Ted and Betsy Lewin
- ❑ Coral Reef
  - *Aquarium Guide*, page 129
  - *Coral Reef* – Barbara Taylor
  - *Down Under Down Under* – Ann McGovern

- ❑ Kangaroo
  - *Zoo Guide*, page 55
  - *Pocket Factfiles: Mammals*, pages 248–249
  - *Magnificent Mammals*, page 56
  - *Cycle of a Kangaroo* – Angela Royston
  - *Young Kangaroo* – Margaret Wise Brown
  - *Kangaroos* – Peter Murray (evolution on page 13)
  - www.enchantedlearning.com/subjects/mammals/marsupial/Kangaroocoloring.shtml
  - www.zooatlanta.org/home/animals/mammals/kangaroo

- ❑ Wombat
  - *Zoo Guide*, page 105
  - *Wombats* – Barbara Triggs
  - *Pocket Factfiles: Mammals*, pages 242–243
  - www.enchantedlearning.com/subjects/mammals/marsupial/Wombatcoloring.shtml

❑ Koala
- *Zoo Guide*, page 57
- *Pocket Factfiles: Mammals*, pages 240–241
- *Magnificent Mammals*, page 38
- *Koalas* – Denise Burt
- www.enchantedlearning.com/themes/koala.shtml
- http://kids.nationalgeographic.com/Animals/CreatureFeature/Koala

❑ Crocodile
- *Zoo Guide*, page 201
- *Crocodiles!* – Irene Trimble
- *I Wonder Why Crocodiles Float Like Logs* – Annabelle Donati

❑ Tasmanian Devil
- *Zoo Guide*, page 93
- *Pocket Factfiles: Mammals*, pages 236–237
- www.enchantedlearning.com/subjects/mammals/marsupial/Tazdevilprintout.shtm
- http://kids.nationalgeographic.com/Animals/CreatureFeature/Tasmanian-devil

❑ Duck-billed Platypus
- *Pocket Factfiles: Mammals*, pages 230–231
- *Magnificent Mammals*, page 46
- www.enchantedlearning.com/subjects/mammals/platypus/Duckbillprintout.shtml

Activities

❑ Color the flag of Australia.

❑ Color or label a map of Australia.

❑ Label the Great Barrier Reef on a world map.

❑ Make Damper Bread.

| 2 cups self-rising flour | 1 cup milk | ½ tsp salt | 1 T butter |

Directions: Sift the flour and salt. Cut in butter. Mix in sufficient milk to form dough. Place on a floured surface and knead lightly. Place the dough into a greased 9″ cake pan. Bake at 350°F for 30–40 minutes until well browned.

❑ Make an Australian meal from *Eat Your Way Around the World.*

❑ For printable color pages and activities go to the www.adc.nsw.gov.au/kids.html website.

Bible

❑ *The Very Boastful Kangaroo*
- Proverbs 25:14
- Proverbs 27:1
- Proverbs 13:10
- James 4:16

Holidays and Celebrations

❑ *Festivals of the World: Australia* – Diana Griffiths

❑ www.atn.com.au/info/holidays.html

❑ http://members.iinet.net.au/~joan/

Travel and Tourism

Australian Tourist Commission
2049 Century Park East, Suite 1920
Los Angeles CA 90067

Telephone: 310-229-4870
Website: www.australia.com

Flag of Australia

Australia

FIND THE TWINS

WHICH TWO ARE EXACTLY ALIKE?

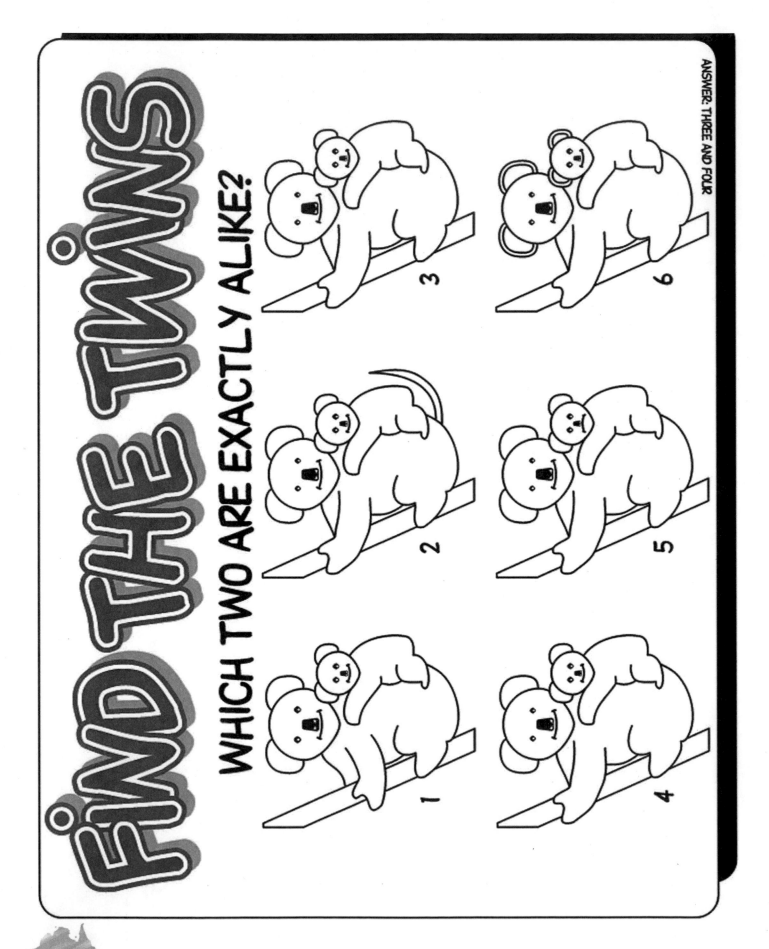

240

Australia

MAZE CRAZE

Start
Here

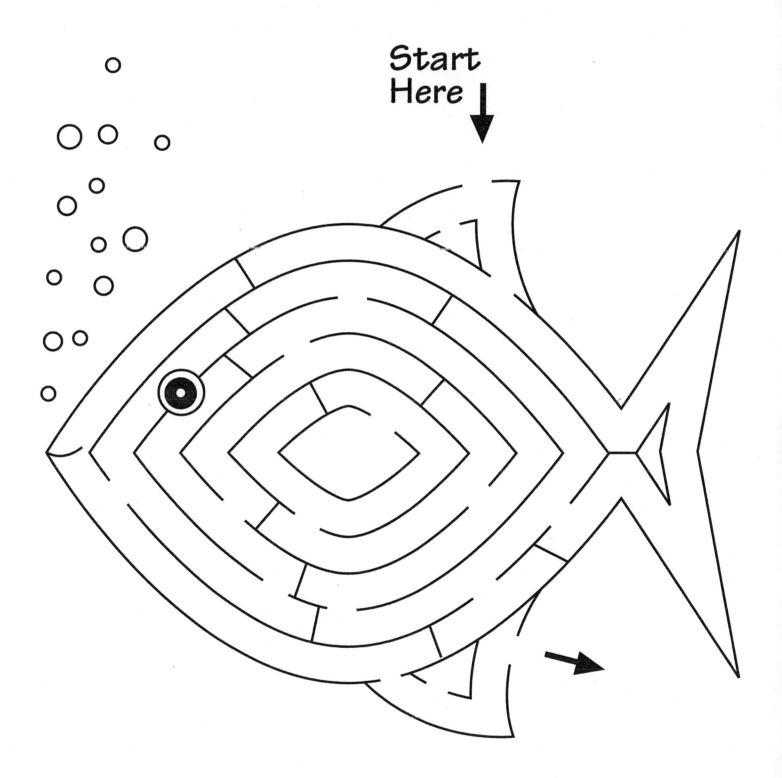

Australia

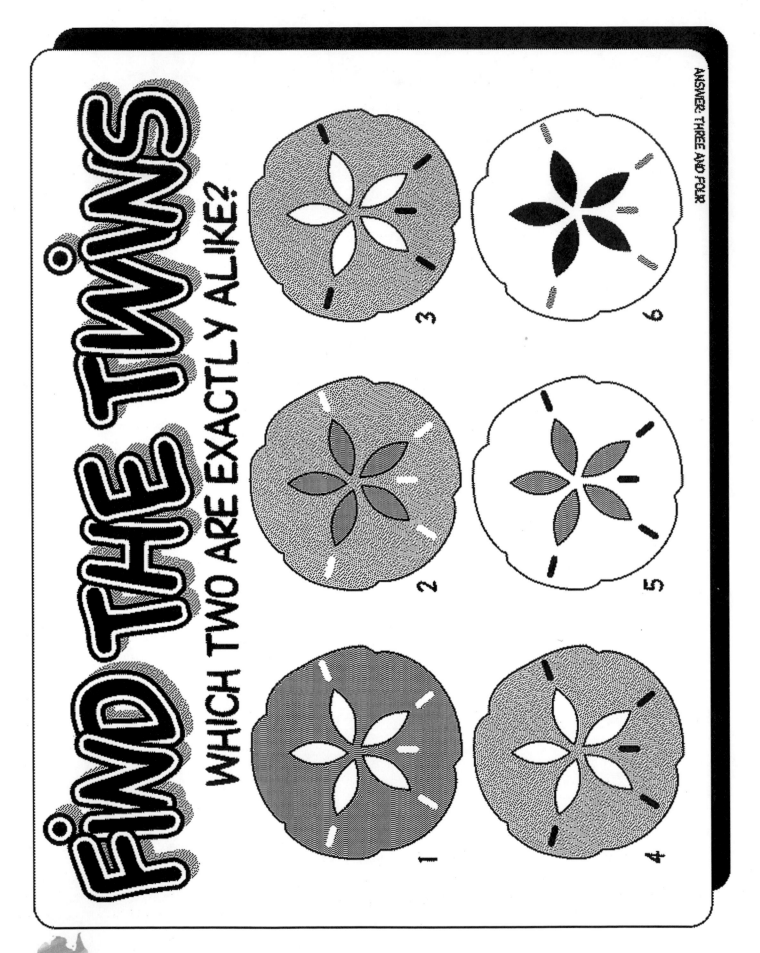

FIND THE TWINS

WHICH TWO ARE EXACTLY ALIKE?

242

Australia

Word Search

```
y u y c g a a z k o j k u t
a u s t r a l i a u r n o a
z c g o y d o q t h y q a s
j k c c r o c o d i l e a m
j a c l x g h f z w l k c a
t n j i k q v f j o a u x n
u g r r o d j d n m h p v i
r a u w a c r b x b y k p a
n r e w l o e i e a c k p n
f o i z a v o t f t s j x d
g o k c o r a l r e e f f e
n s o g r o l i d o i k s v
h p l a t y p u s n z n p i
a b o r i g i n e a z y m l
```

aborigine
Australia
coral reef
crocodile
kangaroo

Australia

koala
platypus
tasmanian devil
wombat

243

New Zealand

Population _____

Capital City _____

Religion _____

Type of Government _____

Currency _____

Language _____

What are the people called? _____

244

New Zealand

Made up of two larger islands and several smaller ones, New Zealand belongs to an island group known as Polynesia. The two larger islands are known simply as North Island and South Island. New Zealand is about the size of Colorado. The capital is Wellington.

The flag of New Zealand is a field of blue with the Union Jack of the United Kingdom in the upper, right corner and four red stars outlined in white representing the Southern Cross. The flag was adopted in 1902.

The islands that make up New Zealand are narrow and no place is more than 80 miles from the coast. New Zealand is very mountainous. Mountains and hills are always within view.

Geography
❑ Island
    • *Geography from A to Z,* page 24

History and Biographies
❑ Margaret Mahy (author from New Zealand)
    • *My Mysterious World* – Margaret Mahy
❑ Maori
    • www.maori.org.nz

General References
❑ *Take a Trip to New Zealand* – Geoff Burns
❑ *New Zealand* – Akinobu Yanagi
❑ *Children Just Like Me,* pages 74–75

Literature
❑ *Missionary Stories with the Millers,* chapter 6
❑ *The Rattlebang Picnic* – Margaret Mahy
❑ *The Great White Man-Eating Shark* – Margaret Mahy
❑ *17 Kings and 42 Elephant* – Margaret Mahy
❑ *A Summery Saturday Morning* – Margaret Mahy

LanguageArts

❑ Choose from the Language Arts Suggestions on page 6.

❑ Make an acronym of New Zealand. Have the child come up with a fact about the country for each letter of its name.

❑ Make a bound book of vegetables and write adjectives describing those vegetables. Refer to the *Big Book of Books and Activities,* page 50.

Science

❑ Fruits and Vegetables
- *Cool as a Cucumber, Hot as a Pepper* – Meredith Sayles Hughes
- *Eat the Fruit, Plant the Seed* – Millicent E. Selsam
- *Eating the Alphabet* – Lois Ehlert
- *What's In the Names of Fruit* – Peter Limburg
- *Growing Food* – Claire Llewellyn
- www.enchantedlearning.com
- www.crayola.com/activitybook/
- *Usborne Internet-linked Science Encyclopedia,* pages 274–279

❑ Kiwi
- www.enchantedlearning.com/subjects/birds/printouts/Kiwiprintout.shtml

❑ Kunekune Pig
- www.zooatlanta.org/home/animals/mammals/kunekune_pigs

Activities

❑ Color the flag of New Zealand.

❑ Color the map of New Zealand.

❑ Label the Tasman Sea on a world map.

❑ Make Kumara and Apple Casserole.

4 boiled sweet potatoes, peeled and cubed	½ cup brown sugar
4 apples, peeled, cored, thinly sliced	½ teaspoon salt
4 tablespoons butter	

Directions: Gently mix first four ingredients in a large bowl. Transfer to baking dish and dot with butter. Bake in a 350°F oven for 1 hour. Serve as a side dish or dessert.

❑ Make Rock Cakes.

1 cup all-purpose flour	½ teaspoon salt
½ cup each butter, sugar, raisins	2 tablespoons orange marmalade
1 egg, lightly beaten	

Directions: Mix flour and salt in mixing bowl, blend in butter until like fine bread crumbs. Add sugar, raisins, and marmalade, mix well with spoon. Add egg until mixture is stiff and "rocky." Pull off golf ball-sized chunks of dough and place on cookie sheet 1-inch apart. Bake in 425°F oven for 15 minutes. Remove from cookie sheet. Turn cakes upside down to cool. Serve with tea.

❑ Make a New Zealand meal from *Eat Your Way Around the World.*

Bible

- ❑ Fruits and Vegetables
  - Genesis 1:9–13
  - Genesis 3
  - Genesis 4:1–15
  - Psalm 1
  - Matthew 7:15–20
  - Mark 4:1–20
  - John 15:1–8
  - Galatians 5:22–23
- ❑ *The Rattlebang Picnic*
  - Psalm 127:3
- ❑ *The Great White Man-Eating Shark*
  - Proverbs 21:26
  - Isaiah 56:11

Holidays and Celebrations

- ❑ www.ers.dol.govt.nz/holidays_act_2003/dates/
- ❑ www.teara.govt.nz/1966/H/HolidaysPublic/HolidaysPublic/en/
- ❑ www.experiencenz.com/dates.cfm

Travel and Tourism

Tourism New Zealand
Suite 1904
780 3rd Avenue
New York, NY 10017-2024

Telephone: 1-866-639-9325 (toll-free in USA and Canada)
Telephone: 212-832-8482

Email: nzinfo@nztb.govt.nz

Website: www.newzealand.com/travel/

Flag of New Zealnad

New Zealand

248

FIND THE TWINS

WHICH TWO ARE EXACTLY ALIKE?

ANSWER: ONE AND THREE

3

6

2

5

1

4

249

New Zealand

Oceania Review Map

See how many countries you can identify. Write their names on the map.

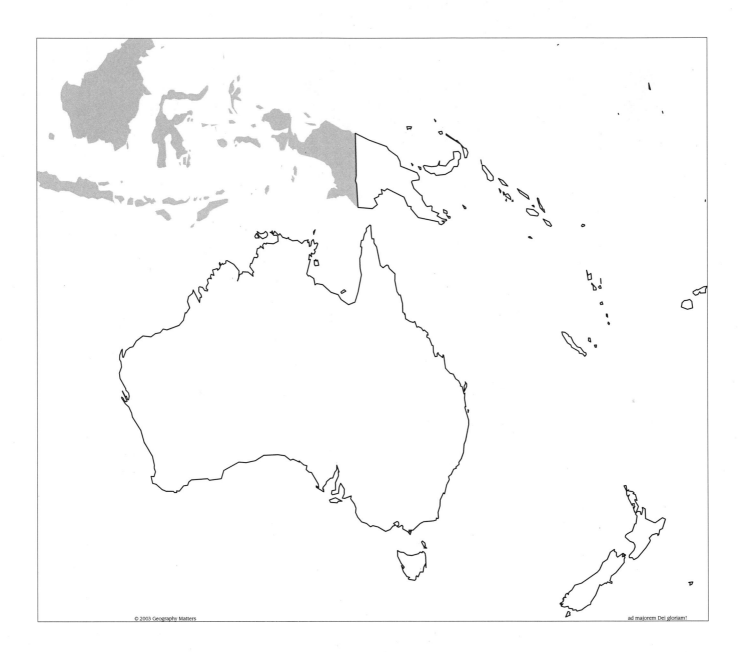

© 2003 Geography Matters   ad majorem Dei gloriam!

Appendix

Appendix

Making 3-D Maps

Materials: cookie dough or clay recipe, waxed paper, blue icing, green sprinkles, clear sprinkles, small chocolate chips, red candy strips (licorice strings), M&Ms®.

1. Tape or trace an outline map of the area on the cardboard for accuracy in forming the general shape of the state or region. Use toothpicks with

2. Using a physical map from in your student atlas, place the dough or clay on the cardboard and shape like the state or region you are studying.

3. Use toothpicks with flags to label the capital, rivers, mountain ranges, etc. and push into map before it dries, or leave unlabeled.

If using salt dough, let dry overnight and paint, if desired.

Traditional Salt Dough

2 parts flour

1 part salt Mix well.

1 part water

Directions: Mix well. Add more water if crumbly.

Cookie Dough

Dough Recipe:

2 cups smooth peanut butter   2½ cups powdered sugar

2½ cups powdered milk   2 cups white corn syrup

Directions: Mix all ingredients together and put small portions on waxed paper.

Use these symbols:

blue icing – lakes and oceans   **clear sprinkles** – deserts   **red candy strips** – rivers

green sprinkles – plains   **chocolate chips** – mountains   **M&Ms®** – capitals

**The above information was taken from the www.geomatters.com and www.tapestryofgrace.com websites.

Dictionary

word

Draw a picture of what your word means.

Biography Report

What is my name? _____

When was I born? _____ When did I die? _____

Where did I live? _____

Who were my parents? _____

How many brothers and sisters did I have? _____

Who did I marry? _____

How many children did we have? _____

What kind of work did I do? _____

_____

Why am I important? _____

_____

_____

What mistakes did I make? _____

_____

_____

What did you learn from me? _____

_____

_____

Country Report

Country: _____

Continent: _____

Capital: _____

Language: _____   Put a picture here

What kind of houses do the people live in? _____

_____

What kind of food do the people eat? _____

_____

Geographical features: mountains   deserts   plains   coast

Climate: hot   cold   moderate   tropical

Major rivers and lakes: _____

Famous people: _____

_____

Animals: _____

_____

Would you like to visit this country?   Yes   No

Why? _____

_____

Animal Report

Name of the animal: _____

Where does the animal live? _____

What is its home like? _____

_____

What does it eat? _____

_____

This animal is awake during the: Day   Night

What kind of climate does this animal like? _____

_____

What special features did God give this animal? _____

_____

_____

Draw a picture of this animal.

Appendix

Answer Keys

Page : 18
1. North America
2. South America
3. Europe
4. Asia
5. Africa
6. Australia
7. Antartcica

Page : 71

Across
2. Sherwood
3. Thames
4. Big Ben
5. petrol
6. mate
8. Elizabeth

Down
1. London
2. Shakespeare
7. sheep

Page : 78

Across
1. Paris
5. Eiffel Tower
6. Joan
7. Curie

Down
1. perfume
2. Monet
3. Pasteur
4. French

Page : 88

Across
1. Venus
3. Mars
4. Uranus
7. Milky Way
8. Jupiter
9. Saturn
10. Mercury
12. asteroid
13. planet
14. comet

Down
2. Neptune
3. moon
5. solar system
6. star
11. earth
13. Pluto

Page : 110
1. Spanish or Spaniard
2. Spanish
3. Portugese
4. Portugese

Page : 126
1. North America
2. Asia
3. Europe

Page : 144

Across
2. horse
4. cat
6. duck
9. rooster
10. pig

Down
1. chicken
3. sheep
4. cow
5. turkey
7. dog

Page : 156

Across
6. Mississippi
8. Columbus
11. Hawaii
12. Lincoln
14. Georgia
15. Kentucky

Down
1. Arizona
2. Washington
3. Virginia
4. Missouri
5. Texas
7. Delaware
9. fifty
10. Florida
13. New jersey

Page : 165

Across
3. ocho
5. sies
8. cuatro
9. dies

Down
1. tres
2. uno
4. cinco
6. siete
7. nueve
9. dos

Page : 203

Across
3. ape
4. gorilla
6. monkey
9. chimp
10. hippo

Down
1. zebra
2. giraffe
5. lion
7. ostrich
8. rhino

259

Appendix

Word Search Answers

Page 19
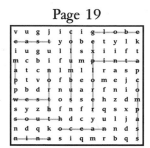

Page 111

Page 159
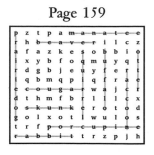

Page 20

Page 125
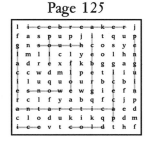

Page 166
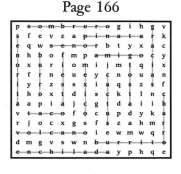

Page 55

Page 130
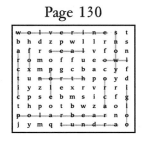

Page 172
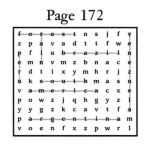

Page 87
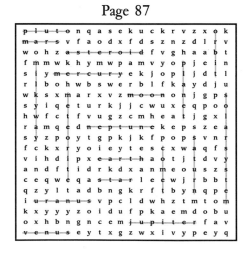

Page 145
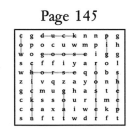

Page 204

Page 158
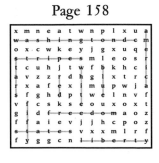

Page 243
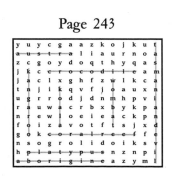

Appendix

Index

OTHER PRODUCTS PUBLISHED BY GEOMATTERS

Trail Guide to Geography Series
by Cindy Wiggers

The *Trail Guide to Geography* series is a multi-level geography curriculum guide for elementary grades through High School. Three books in the *Trail Guide to ...Geography* series include U.S., World, and Bible geography. Each book provides clear directions and assignment choices to encourage self-directed learning as students create their own personal geography notebooks. Daily atlas drills, mapping activities, and various weekly assignment choices address learning styles in a way that has kids asking for more!

Trail Guide features:
- Weekly lesson plans – for 36 weeks
- 5-minute daily atlas drills (2 questions/day, four days/week)
- 3 levels of difficulty – all ages participate together
- Weekly mapping assignments
- A variety of weekly research and hands-on activity choices

Student Notebooks are available as a digital download.

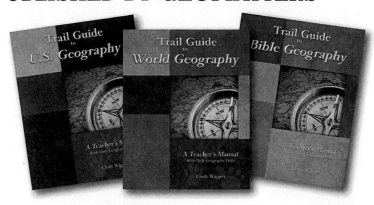

Trail Guide Levels
The *Trail Guide* Levels are just a guide. Select a level according to student ability, and match level with the appropriate atlas or student notebook.

- Elementary: grades 2–4
- Middle School: grades 5–8
- High School

All 3 levels in each book!

Note: Elementary is ideal for independent 3rd and 4th graders. Second graders will need plenty of guidance. If your oldest is 2nd–3rd grade range, please consider *Galloping the Globe* or *Cantering the Country* first.

Trail Guide to U.S. Geography
Grades 2 - 12

"The *Trail Guide to U.S. Geography* provides lots of guidance while allowing for (and encouraging) flexibility and this is just the balance most homeschool moms need! The manual is easy to navigate and I am very impressed with how thoroughly material is covered. This resource is destined to be a favorite with homeschool families for years to come!"
–Cindy Prechtel, homeschoolingfromtheheart.com

Trail Guide to World Geography
Grades 2 - 12

"We have the *Trail Guide to World Geography* and **love** it!! We are using it again this year just for the questions... I will never sell this guide!! I am looking forward to doing the U.S. one next year."
–Shannon, OK

Trail Guide to Bible Geography
Grades 2 - 12

"Here is another winner from Geography Matters! *Trail Guide to Bible Geography* is multi-faceted, user-friendly, and suited to a wide range of ages and abilities."
–Jean Hall, Eclectic Homeschool Association

Galloping the Globe
Grades K - 4
by Loreé Pettit and Dari Mullins

"If you've got kindergarten through fourth grade students, and are looking for unit study material for geography, hold on to your hat and get ready for *Galloping the Globe!* Loreé Pettit and Dari Mullins have written this great resource to introduce children to the continents and some of their countries. This book is designed to be completed in one to three years, depending on how much time you spend on each topic. And for each continent, there are suggestions and topics galore." –Leslie Wyatt, www.homeschoolenrichment.com

Organized by continent, incorporates student notebooking, and covers these topics:

- **Basic Geography**
- **History and Biographies**
- **Literature**
- **Science**
- **Bible**
- **Activities**
- **Internet Sources**
- **Language Arts**

Includes an Activity CD-ROM jam-packed with all the reproducible activity sheets found in the book plus added bonus pages.

Cantering the Country
Grades 1–5
by Loreé Pettit and Dari Mullins

Saddle up your horses and strap on your thinking caps. Learning geography is an adventure. From the authors who brought you *Galloping the Globe,* you'll love its U.S. counterpart, *Cantering the Country.* This unit study teaches a wide range of academic and spiritual disciplines using the geography of the U.S. as a starting point. With this course, you won't have to put aside one subject to make time for another. They're all connected! This comprehensive unit study takes up to three years to complete and includes all subjects except math and spelling. Incorporates student notebooking and covers these topics:

- **U.S. Geography**
- **Character**
- **Science**
- **Language Arts**
- **Activities**
- **Literature**
- **Civics**
- **History and Biographies**
- **Internet Sources**

This book includes a CD-ROM packed full of reproducible outline maps and activities. Dust off your atlas and get ready to explore America!

OTHER PRODUCTS PUBLISHED BY GEOMATTERS

Adventures of Munford Series
by Jamie Aramini

Although he's just two parts hydrogen and one part oxygen, Munford is all adventure. He can be rain, snow, sleet, or steam. He has traveled the world in search of excitement. Throughout history, he has been present at some of the most important and world-changing events.

Fun and educational, Munford will inspire your children to learn more about many of history's greatest events. These readers make a great addition to your learning experience in areas such as history, geography, and science. This book series was written on an elementary reading level, but provides plenty of read-aloud entertainment for the entire family!

The American Revolution

In this adventure, Munford travels to colonial America and experiences first-hand the events leading to the American Revolution. He meets famed American Founding Fathers, such as Samuel Adams, Thomas Jefferson, and George Washington. He joins the Sons of Liberty under cover of night to dump tea into Boston Harbor. He tags along for Paul Revere's most famous ride, and even becomes a part of the Declaration of Independence in a way that you might not expect!

The Klondike Gold Rush

In this adventure, Munford finds himself slap into the middle of the Klondike Gold Rush. He catches gold fever on this dangerous, yet thrilling, adventure. Meet some of the Gold Rush's most famous characters, like gold baron Alex McDonald or the tricky villain named Soapy Smith. Take a ride on the Whitehorse Rapids, and help Munford as he pans for gold. This is an adventure you won't soon forget!

Munford Meets Lewis & Clark

Join Munford on an epic adventure with Meriwether Lewis and William Clark, as they make their perilous journey in search of the Northwest Passage to the Pacific Ocean.

Munford Meets Robert Fulton

Join Munford— the world's most daring water molecule in his latest adventure! Munford joins forces with Robert Fulton, inventor of the world's first practical steam boat!

Eat Your Way Through the USA
by Loreé Pettit

Taste your way around the U.S.A. without leaving your own dining room table! Each state has its unique geographical features, culinary specialities, and agricultural products. These influence both the ingredients that go into a recipe and the way food is prepared. Compliment your geography lesson and tantalize your tastebuds at the same time with this outstanding cookbook.

This cookbook includes a full meal of easy to follow recipes from each state. Though they aren't written at a child's level, it's easy to include your students in the preparation of these dishes. Cooking together provides life skills and is a source of bonding and pride. More than just a cookbook, it is a taste buds-on approach to geography.

Eat Your Way Around the World
by Jamie Aramini

Get out the sombrero for your Mexican fiesta! Chinese egg rolls… corn pancakes from Venezuela… fried plantains from Nigeria. All this, and more, is yours when you take your family on a whirlwind tour of over thirty countries in this unique international cookbook. Includes a full meal of recipes from each country. Recipes are easy to follow, and ingredients are readily available. Jam-packed with delicious dinners, divine drinks, and delectable desserts, this book is sure to please.

The entire family will be fascinated with tidbits of culture provided for each country including: Etiquette Hints, Food Profiles, and Culture a la Carté. For more zest, add an activity and violà, create a memorable learning experience that will last for years to come. Some activities include: Food Journal, Passport, and World Travel Night.

The Ultimate Geography and Timeline Guide
by Maggie Hogan and Cindy Wiggers

Grades K - 12

Learn how to construct timelines, establish student notebooks, teach geography through literature, and integrate science with activities on volcanoes, archaeology, and other subjects. Use the complete multi-level geography course for middle and high school students. Includes a digital download of all reproducible activity and planning pages. Use for all students kindergarden through high school.

- 18 Reproducible Outline Maps
- Teaching Tips
- Planning Charts
- Over 150 Reproducible Pages
- Over 300 Timeline Figures
- Lesson Plans
- Scope and Sequence
- Flash Cards
- Games

Mark-It Timeline of History

There's hardly no better way to keep history in perspective than creating a timeline in tandem with your history studies. This poster is just the tool to do so. Write or draw images of events as they are studied, or attach timeline figures to aid student understanding and comprehension of the topic at hand. 23" x 34".

800.426.4650   **Geography Matters®**   **www.geomatters.com**

OTHER PRODUCTS PUBLISHED BY GEOMATTERS

Lewis & Clark - Hands On
Art and English Activities
by Sharon Jeffus

Follow the experiences of Meriwether Lewis and William Clark with hands-on art and writing projects associated with journal entries made during the Corps of Discovery Expedition. Ideal for adding interest to any Lewis and Clark study or to teach drawing and journaling. Includes profiles of American artists, step by step drawing instructions, actual journal entries, and background information about this famous adventure.

Geography Through Art
by Sharon Jeffus and Jamie Aramini

Geography Through Art is the ultimate book of international art projects. Join your children on an artistic journey to more than twenty-five countries spanning six continents (includes over a dozen United States projects). Previously published by Visual Manna as *Teaching Geography Through Art*, Geography Matters has added a number of enhancements and practical changes to this fascinating art book. Use this book as an exciting way to supplement any study of geography, history, or social studies. You'll find yourself reaching for this indispensable guide again and again to delight and engage students in learning about geography through the culture and art of peoples around the world.

Profiles from History
by Ashley (Strayer) Wiggers

When studying history, a human connection is the most important connection that we can make.

Profiles from History takes a fresh look a familiar faces. Along with beautiful illustrations and fascinating stories, each book encourages children to think about the motivations of eighteen to twenty historical figures. Activities, timeline figures, and discussion questions help students recognize the effect these individuals have had on history.

Timeline Figures on CD-ROM

Kids love the look of their timelines when they add color and variety. Students can draw on their timeline, write events and dates, and add timeline figures. We've created two different sets of color timeline figures that are ready to print from any computer. There are over 350 figures in each set plus templates to create your own. Our figures are appealing in style, simple to use, and include color-coding and icons to aid memory. Available with biblical events and general world events.

- Reproducible Outline Maps -

Reproducible outline maps have a myriad of uses in the home, school, and office. Uncle Josh's quality digital maps provide opportunities for creative learning at all ages. His maps feature rivers and grid lines where possible, and countries are shown in context with their surroundings. (No map of Germany "floating" in the center of the page, here!) When students use outline maps and see the places they are studying in context they gain a deeper understanding of the subject at hand.

Uncle Josh's Outline Map Book

Take advantage of those spontaneous teaching moments when you have this set of outline maps handy. They are:

- Over 100 reproducible maps
- 15 world regions
- Continents with and without borders
- 25 countries
- Each of the 50 United States
- 8 U.S. regions

Useful for all grades and topics, this is by far one of the best book of reproducible outline maps you'll find.

Uncle Josh's Outline Map Collection CD-ROM

In addition to all maps in *Uncle Josh's Outline Map Book* the CD-Rom includes color, shaded-relief, and labeled maps. Over 260 printable maps plus bonus activities.

- Large-scale Maps -

Large-scale maps are great for detail labeling and for family or classroom use. Laminated Mark-It maps can be reused for a variety of lessons. Quality digital map art is used for each of the map titles published and laminated by Geography Matters. Choose from large scale continents, regions, United States, and world maps. US and World available in both outline version and with state, country, and capitals labeled. Ask about our ever expanding library of full, color shaded-relief maps. Paper and laminated, each title available separately or in discounted sets.

OTHER PRODUCTS PUBLISHED BY GEOMATTERS

Trail Guide to Learning

Children learn best when learning overlaps and builds upon a main concept. The **Trail Guide to Learning** series is a complete homeschool curriculum that teaches every subject except for math. We not only cover each subject, but every topic in the Trail Guide relates. It is a natural way of learning as subjects flow from one to the other.

Weaving together aspects from Charlotte Mason's methods of natural education, incorporating the ideas of Dr. Benjamin Bloom's research on thinking skills, and utilizing the time-tested approach developed by noted author and educator, Dr. Ruth Beechick you can make learning both long term and enjoyable.

Exploration is the first step in the Trail Guide to Learning series. Learn about the character and experiences of explorers from Columbus to those who opened the way westward. These brave individuals shaped us as a nation with their vision, determination, and sacrifice. Intended for grades 3-5 with a younger extension available for grades K-2 and an older extension for grades 6-7.

Settlement is next. Study the accomplishments of great Americans like George Washington and Abraham Lincoln, who built upon the trail blazed by the explorers. Their actions teach us the principles of freedom and citizenship. From the Revolutionary War to the Civil War, learn how our country was established. Intended for grades 4-6 with an extension available for grades 7-8.

Progress is the third step of our American History series. To grow as a country, another group of leaders had to step forward during our history—scientists and inventors. The lives of these devoted individuals and their contributions will be examined throughout our history, into the Industrial Revolution and the beginning of the 20th century. Intended for grades 5-7 with an extension available for grades 8-9.

When students understand the foundation of service, leadership, and the principles of freedom that this country was built upon, they have a frame of reference and can accurately compare our nation to others throughout history. That is why our world history series, *Journeys*, comes *after* the Paths of American History.

Journeys Through the Ancient World is the fourth step in the **Trail Guide to Learning** series. This level of the curriculum will transport your students into four important early civilizations—Egypt, Israel, Greece, and Rome. Astronomy, worldview comparisons, typing, Hebrew, geography, and language skills are included in each of four, nine-week units. The *Bible* is an essential part of this study, as both an historical and a literary text. This full, one-year course is targeted for grades 6-8.

About the Authors

Loreé Pettit is a wife and homeschooling mother to three children. Her background as school teacher and administrator helped her see the value in adapting traditional teaching methods for schooling at home. She developed a love for geography as a child traveling throughout the United States and Europe with her family. In 2001 she translated that interest into a geography-based unit study for her own children. That unit study went into publication the following year as *Galloping the Globe. Eat your Way through the USA* and *Cantering the Country* soon followed.

When she is not writing, or involved with the many details of teaching her own children, Loreé presents workshops at home school conferences across the country. There, she helps parents realize that home schooling is more than bringing traditional teaching methods into the home. Her heart is to help parents discover the joys of learning together as a family.

Dari Mullins, author and motivational speaker, has been homeschooling her three teenagers for over ten years. She fell in love with history and geography when she began researching home education in 1995. Dari and her husband, Allen, have taught their children at home since the oldest started kindergarten in 1997.

Realizing early that traditional textbooks were not the route she wanted in educating her children, Dari utilized notebooking and the unit study approach. This passion for non-traditional methods led her to write curriculum for her own family and eventually teaming up with Loree Pettit to write *Galloping the Globe* and *Cantering the Country*.

Dari and her family currently live in Asheville, NC where she teaches several classes and stays active with the local homeschool community. She remains dedicated to helping homeschool families prosper and delight in learning together.